SCRIPTURE & THE MYSTERY OF
THE MASS

For as often as you eat this bread and drink the cup,
you proclaim the Lord's death until he comes.
1 Corinthians 11:26

SCRIPTURE & THE MYSTERY OF
THE MASS

Edited by
Scott Hahn and Regis J. Flaherty

With a Foreword by
Bishop Robert C. Morlino

EMMAUS
ROAD
PUBLISHING

Emmaus Road Publishing
1468 Parkview Circle
Steubenville, Ohio 43952

Library of Congress Control Number: 2004104786
ISBN: 978-1-941447-42-0

Cover design by
Margaret Ryland

Editorial Assistance by
Mary Wake and Carrie Cusick

Nihil Obstat: Rev. James Dunfee, *Censor Librorum*
Imprimatur: ✠ R. Daniel Conlon, D.D., J.C.D., Ph.D, Bishop of Steubenville
Date: April 22, 2004

The *Nihil Obstat* and *Imprimatur* are official declarations
that a book or pamphlet is free of doctrinal or moral error.
No implication is contained therein that those who have
granted the *Nihil Obstat* and *Imprimatur* agree with
the contents, opinions, or statements expressed.

CONTENTS

Foreword

Our Holy Father has on many occasions distinguished human persons from the rest of God's marvelous creation by our capacity for wonder. It is this wonder that ultimately leads human reason to faith in Jesus Christ. This wonder is most activated in our humanity when we receive the gift of the Lord Himself—His Body, His Blood—under the signs of bread and wine at the Eucharistic sacrifice and celebration. It is quite predictable that our Holy Father would focus on *amazement* as the appropriate response of the believer to Christ's presence in the Eucharist.

A culture of death is frequently a culture of cynicism, where belief in miracles is considered unsophisticated and unworthy of contemporary enlightened people. And yet the Eucharistic miracle is the greatest miracle of all. If we exercise our capacity for wonder and therein discover the depths of our own humanity, we really find fulfillment, then, in amazement at the truth of Christ's presence in the Eucharist.

In speaking, especially with young people, about this amazement, which our Holy Father describes in his encyclical *Ecclesia de Eucharistia*, I have invited and exhorted them to reclaim the "WOW" of our faith. That Christ would be completely present to us through the sacramental signs transcends our highest hopes for intervention by God in daily human life. In comparison to this Eucharistic presence and reality, all other miracles pale. If we arrive for the Eucharistic sacrifice and celebration, bringing along with us this "WOW" in the depth of our hearts, there will be no such thing as a Eucharistic Liturgy that is not meaningful, no matter what human failings or flaws might accompany it. The Mass celebrated according to the mind of the Church, even when there are distractions or imperfections as the rite is carried out, still energizes and realizes the "WOW" in the heart of the believer.

How does one nourish this "WOW" outside the celebration of Mass so as to bring it to the Mass "polished up" and at its very best? In *Ecclesia de Eucharistia*, the Holy Father strongly invites us to the practice of Eucharistic adoration outside of Mass, before Christ's presence in the tabernacle. Deacon Owen Cummings, Professor of Liturgical Theology at Mount Angel Seminary in Portland, Oregon, has spoken of Eucharistic adoration before the tabernacle as the Mass in meditation. It is the prolongation of the sacrificial banquet, which takes place at the altar. The Eucharistic presence in the tabernacle comes *from the altar* and sustains our "WOW," so that we might return *to the altar* truly prepared to offer with

Christ, the only High Priest, the one eternal sacrifice of praise.

This third volume of the *"Catholic for a Reason"* series will provide for the reader much food for prayerful reflection, much of which will, I hope, take place before the tabernacle. The content of this volume will surely nourish the "WOW," which should abide in the heart of every disciple of Christ, so that our amazement in the face of the Eucharistic mystery, as well as our human capacity for wonder, might be stirred. After all, to be human is to be like Christ—to find our redeemed self, our best face, as *we look into His face*, the face of Him who encourages us when we are sad and strengthens us when we are joyful. As the Second Vatican Council has taught us, the Eucharist is the source and the summit of our life as followers of Christ. We should, then, examine our conscience about our capacity for the "WOW," for amazement and wonder, and do everything to nurture those wonderful gifts of the Father, the Son, and the Holy Spirit. *Catholic for a Reason III: Scripture and the Mystery of the Mass* will serve to enliven these marvelous gifts so that, through the Eucharist, we might become more truly human—that is more truly holy, more truly like Christ.

† MOST REV. ROBERT C. MORLINO
Bishop of Madison

Abbreviations

Joel	Joel
Amos	Amos
Obad.	Obadiah
Jon.	Jonah
Mic.	Micah
Nahum	Nahum
Hab.	Habakkuk
Zeph.	Zephaniah
Hag.	Haggai
Zech.	Zechariah
Mal.	Malachi
1 Mac.	1 Maccabees
2 Mac.	2 Maccabees

THE NEW TESTAMENT

Mt.	Matthew
Mk.	Mark
Lk.	Luke
Jn.	John
Acts	Acts of the Apostles
Rom.	Romans
1 Cor.	1 Corinthians
2 Cor.	2 Corinthians
Gal.	Galatians
Eph.	Ephesians
Phil.	Philippians
Col.	Colossians
1 Thess.	1 Thessalonians
2 Thess.	2 Thessalonians
1 Tim.	1 Timothy
2 Tim.	2 Timothy
Tit.	Titus
Philem.	Philemon
Heb.	Hebrews
Jas.	James
1 Pet.	1 Peter

2 Pet.	2 Peter
1 Jn.	1 John
2 Jn.	2 John
3 Jn.	3 John
Jude	Jude
Rev.	Revelation (Apocalypse)

DOCUMENTS OF VATICAN II

SC — Constitution on the Sacred Liturgy (*Sacrosanctum Concilium*), December 4, 1963

IM — Decree on the Means of Social Communication (*Inter Mirifica*), December 4, 1963

LG — Dogmatic Constitution on the Church (*Lumen Gentium*), November 21, 1964

OE — Decree on the Catholic Eastern Churches (*Orientalium Ecclesiarum*), November 21, 1964

UR — Decree on Ecumenism (*Unitatis Redintegratio*), November 21, 1964

CD — Decree on the Pastoral Office of Bishops in the Church (*Christus Dominus*), October 28, 1965

PC — Decree on the Up-to-Date Renewal of Religious Life (*Perfectae Caritatis*), October 28, 1965

OT — Decree on the Training of Priests (*Optatam Totius*), October 28, 1965

GE — Declaration on Christian Education (*Gravissimum Educationis*), October 28, 1965

NA — Declaration on the Relation of the Church to Non-Christian Religions (*Nostra Aetate*), October 28, 1965

DV — Dogmatic Constitution on Divine Revelation (*Dei Verbum*), November 18, 1965

AA	Decree on the Apostolate of Lay People (*Apostolicam Actuositatem*), November 18, 1965
DH	Declaration on Religious Liberty (*Dignitatis Humanae*), December 7, 1965
AG	Decree on the Church's Missionary Activity (*Ad Gentes Divinitus*), December 7, 1965
PO	Decree on the Ministry and Life of Priests (*Presbyterorum Ordinis*), December 7, 1965
GS	Pastoral Constitution on the Church in the Modern World (*Gaudium et Spes*), December 7, 1965

OTHER ABBREVIATIONS

EE	Pope John Paul II, Encyclical on the Eucharist in Its Relationship to the Church *Ecclesia de Eucharistia* (April 17, 2003)
LXX	The Greek Septuagint
NAB	New American Bible
NJB	New Jerusalem Bible

CHAPTER I

A Biblical Walk
Through the Mass

EDWARD P. SRI

I never realized how Scriptural the Mass was until my first encounter with "Bible Christians."

As a "cradle Catholic," I was quite familiar with the rituals of the Mass. I knew when to stand and when to kneel. I knew when to say, "Amen," and when to say, "And also with you." However, I was never sure about the *meaning* of all these rituals: where they came from, why we did them, and how they led us into a deeper relationship with Christ.

After I went away to college, this lack of understanding about the Mass came back to haunt me, especially when I came across, for the first time in my life, self-professed "Bible Christians." Repeatedly, my Protestant evangelical friends challenged me about my Catholic faith. In particular, they often drilled me about the Mass, saying: "You Catholics have all these pre-fabricated, ritual prayers in the Mass. Why don't you speak to God as a friend and pray to Him from your heart? Our worship should be based on Scripture, so why does the Mass have all these man-made rituals and traditions? Why do Catholics call the Mass a sacrifice? Christ died once and for all. We don't need to sacrifice Him all over again."

At the time, I did not know how to answer my friends' concerns about the Mass. But their good questions led me to dig deeper into the faith of my youth and to explore in greater depth the meaning of the Eucharist. In the process, I discovered great treasures in the Mass, which I had never even known existed.

Most notably, I began to understand just how biblical the Mass really is. I came to see how practically every prayer, hymn, response, and ritual action is saturated with images, themes, and quotes from Sacred Scripture. At almost every point of the Mass, God's Word is jumping out in signs, gestures, words, and songs!

In this chapter, I will explore just a few of those liturgical prayers from the Mass and discuss their Scriptural roots. In the process, I hope that these biblical foundations will help us gain deeper insights into our worship of God and an even greater appreciation for the splendor of the Mass.

Sign, Sealed, Delivered: The Sign of the Cross

Let us begin with the most basic ritual that comes at the opening and closing of every Mass: the sign of the cross. While tracing a cross over our bodies, we say, "*In the name of the Father, and of the Son, and of the Holy Spirit.*" This simple prayer, however, is no empty ritual. In making the sign of the cross, we are performing a sacred biblical action. We are *calling on the name of the Lord*.

Whenever someone calls on the Lord's name in the Bible, it is a powerful moment. Throughout salvation history, when people make or renew their covenant with God, they call on His holy name in order to invite God to act in their lives and to express their firm commitment to live in covenant with Him (e.g., Gen. 4:26; 12:8; 26:25; 1 Kings 18:24, 32). Following this Biblical approach to worship, Catholics begin each Mass by invoking the name of the Triune God: Father, Son, and Holy Spirit. In so doing, we invite the Almighty God into our lives and dedicate all that we do in the Mass to His sacred name.

Furthermore, the ritual action itself of making the sign of the cross on our foreheads has roots in Sacred Scripture. In the Book of Ezekiel, for example, a cross-shaped symbol served as a sign of divine protection. God gave the prophet Ezekiel a vision about the judgment that would fall upon Jerusalem for its idolatry. In this vision, the faithful Jews who were marked with the Hebrew letter *taw* on their foreheads would be spared when the day of reckoning arrived (Ezek. 9:4). What is significant for our topic is that this Hebrew letter had the shape of a cross. Therefore, already in the Old Testament Book of Ezekiel, being marked with a cross on the forehead symbolized covenant union with God and divine protection.

We find this theme continued in the New Testament. Drawing on the Ezekiel image, the Book of Revelation also describes the faithful servants of God in the New Covenant as being marked with *a seal on their foreheads*. This sign sets them apart as God's people and protects them from the divine judgment that will fall upon the earth (Rev. 7:3).

This helps shed light on the Catholic practice of making the sign of the cross. When we first became Christians, we, too, were marked with the sign of a cross at our baptisms when the priest traced the cross of Christ over our bodies. Therefore, whenever we repeat this basic gesture at Mass, we are retracing the same mark that was placed on us at the beginning of our life in Christ. In so doing, we remind ourselves that we have been set apart by Christ, and we renew our commitment to live in union with Him. As in the time of Ezekiel, the sign of the cross continues to serve as a powerful symbol expressing our covenant with God and His protection over our lives.

Mission Impossible? "The Lord Be with You"

Many Catholics are so familiar with this line from the Mass that they may not appreciate the full force of what these words really mean. This is not just a pious greeting or a religious way of saying, "Welcome!" This is not simply a cue for the laity to respond, "And also with you." From a biblical perspective, these words represent a divine summons, an invitation to a daunting undertaking. If we were ancient Jews who understood what the words, "The Lord be with you," really meant, we probably would be trembling in fear and awe every time we heard these words spoken at Mass.

Throughout the Scriptures, when God calls someone to an important role in His plan of salvation, He gives assurance that He will be with that person. For example, when Moses was called to confront

Pharaoh and lead the people out of slavery in Egypt, he was afraid, felt unsure of his own ability, and tried to persuade God to choose someone else for the job. However, God insisted on Moses' mission and told him, "*I will be with you*" (Ex. 3:12). Similarly, when God commissioned Joshua to lead the people into the Promised Land, He said to him, "[A]s I was with Moses, so *I will be with you*" (Josh. 1:5). When God called Gideon to defend the Israelites from their powerful foreign enemies, the angel told him, "*The LORD is with you*" (Judg. 6:12). When God called the young Virgin Mary to serve in the extraordinary role of being the mother of Israel's messiah, Gabriel said to her, "*[T]he Lord is with you*" (Lk. 1:28). When Jesus commissioned the apostles to evangelize the whole world, He said, "*I am with you always*, to the close of the age" (Mt. 28:20).

Throughout salvation history, these sacred words—"the Lord is with you"—are spoken when God calls people to difficult missions which stretch them well beyond their "comfort zones." They are pushed to the point that they can no longer rely on their own talents, strengths, and abilities, and as a result, they begin to realize, at a more profound level, how much they really need God. It is then that the Lord says He will give them the one thing they will need the most: His presence with them through their many trials and sacrifices.

These same biblical words are repeated to us throughout the Mass. Whenever we hear "The Lord be with you," we should be reminded that we, too, are called to an important mission. Like Moses, Mary, and the apostles, we as Christians are called to serve in God's plan of salvation, bringing the Gospel to the world around us. Such a task will not be easy. Whether as citizens trying to transform our country for Christ, lay people desiring to bring Christian values into the workplace, parents trying to raise godly children, or married people striving to love their spouses with patient, forgiving, selfless love, we at times may feel inadequate, overwhelmed, or not "gifted" enough to carry out our vocation as well we would like. Throughout the Mass, however, we are reminded that we do not face the challenges of our mission alone. We are repeatedly reminded of the one thing that will help us fulfill our vocation the most—the Lord is with us.

The Power of the *Kyrie*: "Lord Have Mercy"

In the introductory rites, we also recite the *Kyrie eleison* (Greek for "Lord, have mercy"). Why do we ask for God's mercy three times at the beginning of Mass? First, we must consider how calling on God for His mercy is an ancient biblical practice. Some psalms cry out for God's mercy in times of suffering (e.g., Ps. 119:77; 123:3). Other psalms ask for God in His mercy to forgive peoples' sins. For example, after King David has committed adultery with Bathsheba and murdered her husband, he eventually humbly admits his guilt. He confesses his horrible actions, repents, and asks God's forgiveness by pouring his heart out to the Lord, saying, "*Have mercy on me*, O God, according to thy steadfast love; according to thy abundant mercy blot out my transgressions. Wash me thoroughly from my iniquity, and cleanse me from my sin!" (Ps. 51:1–2).

In the New Testament, people continue to call on God's mercy in the person of Jesus Christ. For example, in the Gospels, two blind men confidently approach Jesus begging for healing in their lives, saying, "Have mercy on us, Son of David" (Mt. 9:27; 20:30, 31). Others come to Jesus and ask for His mercy upon their loved ones who are suffering, saying, "Have mercy on me, O Lord, Son of David; my daughter is severely possessed by a demon" (Mt. 15:22), or "Lord, have mercy on my son, for he is an epileptic and he suffers terribly" (Mt. 17:15). In each case, when someone calls on His mercy, Jesus responds quickly and performs miraculous deeds in people's lives.

At the *Kyrie* in the Mass, we stand in this biblical tradition of calling on God's mercy for our own lives and the lives of others. In reciting the liturgical responses, "Lord have mercy . . . Christ have mercy . . . Lord have mercy," we become like David, repenting of our sins and asking for God's forgiveness. We become like the blind men begging for Christ to heal our own weaknesses and lack of spiritual vision. We become like the fathers in the Gospel, pleading for Jesus to act in the lives of those we love. In saying *Kyrie eleison* ("Lord, have mercy") at Mass, we humbly entrust our entire lives—all our weaknesses, sins, fears and sufferings—and the lives of those we love, to the merciful heart of Christ. As Catholic author Thomas Howard expressed, this cry for God's mercy sums up all the pleas of a fallen world. He says,

> In the Kyrie . . . we may hear the fathomless cry of the whole race of man ascending to heaven from the depths. Kyrie! goes up from all widows, and all dispossessed and brutalized children, and from all the maimed, and the prisoners and exiles, and from every sick-bed, and indeed from all the wounded

beasts, and, we could believe, from all rivers and seas stained with man's filth and landscapes scarred by his plunder. In the liturgy, somehow, we stand before the Lord *in behalf of* his whole groaning creation. And beyond the liturgy: When we hear the groaning of creation, when we see an animal suffering, or some child or hear an ambulance pass, we say "Kyrie eleison!" as the liturgy has taught us. We are priests, remember, through our Baptism; and one of the tasks of the priest is to intercede for others who don't or can't pray for themselves.[1]

This mystical entrusting of all humanity and indeed, all creation, to the infinite mercy of Christ is what we enter into each time we recite the *Kyrie* in the Mass.

Singing with the Angels: The Gloria

Next, we praise God in a hymn known as the "Gloria," which begins with the words: "Glory to God in the highest, and peace to His people on earth." This opening line parallels the song which the countless host of angels sang in the presence of the shepherds on that first Christmas night: "Glory to God in the highest, and on earth peace among men with whom he is well pleased!" (Lk. 2:14).

Therefore, whenever we sing the "Gloria" at Mass, we are not singing any ordinary hymn. We are singing a song inspired by the angels! Even more, we join the choirs of angels in heaven by singing the same praises that they sang to welcome the Christ child in Bethlehem. And this seems most appropriate, for in the Mass, the Christmas mystery is, in a sense, repeated. The same God, who came down to earth and was

[1] *If Your Mind Wanders at Mass* (Steubenville, OH: Franciscan University Press, 1995), 61.

born a child two thousand years ago, comes down to earth again on our altars at every Mass. Thus, it is fitting that we participate in the heavenly praise, which originally greeted the God-Man in Bethlehem, as we prepare at Mass to welcome the same Christ who humbly comes to us in Holy Communion.

The Greatest Bible Study on Earth: Liturgy of the Word

In Jesus' day, the Jewish synagogue worship involved readings from different parts of their Scriptures based on a three-year cycle. Similarly, each Sunday in the Liturgy of the Word, Catholics hear readings from a broad range of Scripture, covering four major areas of the Bible: the Old Testament, the Psalms, the New Testament letters (or Acts or Revelation) and the Gospels. Like the synagogue liturgy, the biblical readings for Sunday Mass are structured on a three-year cycle that presents an amazing breadth of Scripture. In fact, Catholics attending Mass every Sunday end up hearing almost all of the Bible every three years.

The Story That Shapes Our Lives: The Creed

For some people, the Creed may appear to be simply a list of doctrinal assertions that we reaffirm at Mass—as if every Sunday we are saying to God, "Yes, we still believe all this." However, when we consider the biblical roots of the Creed, we will see that this profession of faith is much more than an affirmation of abstract doctrines, or a summary statement of essential Catholic beliefs; even more profoundly, the

Creed we recite each Sunday is meant to shape our very identity and our daily lives.

"Hear, O Israel: The LORD our God is one LORD; and you shall love the LORD your God with all your heart, and with all your soul, and with all your might" (Deut. 6:4–5). These words represent the Israelite creed of the Old Testament known as the *shema*, which was named after the first word of this passage (*shema* = hear). For the ancient Jews, their creed was much more than a summary of religious beliefs. It was a personal and national mission statement that shaped a Jewish person's identity and worldview. In reciting the *shema*, a Jew was basically saying, "This is who I am: I am not a pagan who worships false gods. I am an Israelite in covenant with the one, true God over all the earth. All that I am and do flows from my relationship with this God."

The *shema* was to be recited several times each day: in the morning, at night, and throughout the daytime hours. It was to be taught to the children, spoken regularly in the home, and written on their doorposts (Deut. 6:7–9). Many Jewish martyrs were even willing to die for the *shema*, as they went to their deaths whispering the words of their creed, "The Lord our God is one . . ."

Living Our "*Shema*"

We must recognize that the Christian creed we recite each Sunday is our *shema*. The Old Testament creed emphasized monotheism (the belief that the God of Israel was the one true God over all humanity). The Christian creed is built upon the *shema*, but deepens our understanding of that one God existing as three divine Persons: Father, Son, and Holy Spirit.

In continuity with the old *shema*, the Christian creed affirms that this one God—the Holy Trinity—is God over the entire human family and is at the center of every human heart's deepest longing.

Do we approach the Creed at Mass with the same devotion that the Jews gave to the *shema*? From a biblical standpoint, we must see that the Creed is much more than a routine statement of faith to be recited on Sundays. More to the heart of the matter, the Creed not only defines *what we believe*; it defines *who we are*. Indeed, it summarizes the story that gives meaning to our lives: the Father sent His Son to die for our sins and poured His Spirit into our hearts that we may be reconciled to Him in the Church.

These basic truths from the Creed are not just abstract principles for our minds to grasp; they are the truths that should mold our hearts and guide our lives. United in Jesus Christ through His Holy Spirit, we sinners have become sons and daughters of the Father. This story of salvation certainly is worth retelling and celebrating on a regular basis! This is why we reaffirm our new identity in Christ each Sunday in the Creed. At this moment in the Mass, we stand up before the entire congregation, and before God, to make this public profession of faith and to recommit ourselves to live out all that the Creed represents in our daily lives.

Biblical Thanksgiving: The Eucharistic Prayers

As we move into the second part of the Mass, known as the Liturgy of the Eucharistic, we encounter a series of prayers that are rooted in traditional biblical piety. The Scriptures and ancient Jewish wor-

ship services are filled with prayers of thanksgiving
for God's goodness, for God's creation, and for His
intervention in the life of Israel. Many Psalms follow
this pattern. For example, Psalm 136 begins, "O give
thanks to the LORD, for he is good, for his steadfast
love endures forever." The psalmist then continues
his prayer of thanksgiving by *praising God for His
creation*—for creating the stars, sun, moon, seas, and
land (Ps. 136:4–9). Next, he turns his attention to
thanking God for rescuing Israel from slavery in Egypt.
In recounting the Exodus story, the Psalm retells
God's mighty deeds: striking down the Egyptian
first-born, bringing Israel out of Egypt, parting the
Red Sea, defeating Pharaoh in the waters, leading the
people in the wilderness, and defending them against
foreign armies (Ps. 136:10–22).

The Jewish people even had a distinct type of sacrifice dedicated specifically to thanksgiving, the *todah*
sacrifice. When someone was saved from persecution,
illness, or death, he would praise God for his deliverance with a thanksgiving sacrifice that served as a new
foundation for that person's life.[2] The person would
invite close friends to participate in this sacrificial rite.
After sacrificing an animal, the participants would eat
a meal with bread and wine. Following the pattern
of the psalms, they would sing a song retelling God's
saving action, thanking the Lord for rescuing them
from death.

The Eucharistic prayers of the Mass stand in continuity with the biblical, Jewish tradition of thanksgiving. In fact, the word "Eucharist" itself means
"thanksgiving." These prayers in the Mass echo themes
developed in the Psalms and expressed by the todah

---

[2] Hartmut Gese, "The Origin of the Lord's Supper," in *Essays on Biblical
Theology*, trans. Keith Crim (Minneapolis: Augsburg, 1981), 129.

sacrifices of Jewish antiquity. Consider, for example, the preface to Eucharistic Prayer II, which the priest recites before singing the "Holy, Holy, Holy":

> Father, it is our duty and our salvation always and everywhere to give you thanks through your beloved Son, Jesus Christ. He is the Word through whom you made the universe, the Savior you sent to redeem us. By the power of the Holy Spirit he took flesh and was born of the Virgin Mary. For our sake he opened his arms on the cross; he put an end to death and revealed the resurrection. In this he fulfilled your will and won for you a holy people.

Notice how the prayer begins explicitly with the theme of thanksgiving: "Father, it is our duty . . . to give you *thanks*." Like the Psalms, this Eucharistic prayer continues *praising God for creating the world* through the Son: "He is the Word through whom you made the universe."

The prayer then focuses attention on *thanking God for rescuing us from death*. Like the psalms and todah rituals, the Eucharistic prayer retells the story of how God saved us: By the power of the Holy Spirit, He became a man, and "[f]or our sake he opened his arms on the cross; he *put an end to death* and revealed the resurrection." By fulfilling the Father's will, Jesus has saved us from sin and death, and in this Eucharistic prayer we thank God that through Christ's redemptive sacrifice, we have become "a holy people."

We see, then, that the Eucharistic prayer embodies the basic elements of biblical thanksgiving: thanking God for who He is, for His creation and for His mighty works of salvation, which are retold in summary fashion. This prayer thus serves as a fitting preface to the new *todah* sacrifice, the Eucharist. Just as the todah sacrifices of old involved a gathering of close friends to thank God for rescuing someone from death and to share a communion meal with bread and wine, so the Eucharistic sacrifice involves a gathering of Christians to thank God for delivering us from death and to share a meal in the form of bread and wine: Jesus' own Body and Blood.

Entering the Heavenly Liturgy: "Holy, Holy, Holy"

Next, the Eucharistic prayer reminds us that the Mass is much more than a human event, taking place in some church here on earth. Ultimately, the Mass is a participation in the heavenly liturgy. This is why the priest says, "And so we join the angels and saints in proclaiming your glory as we say . . ."

> Holy, holy, holy Lord, God of power and might, heaven and earth are full of your glory. Hosanna in the highest. Blessed is he who comes in the name of the Lord. Hosanna in the highest.

The first part of this song is taken not from any ordinary hymnal. Rather, it is patterned after the way the angels and saints worship God in heaven. When the prophet Isaiah had a vision of the Lord in heaven, he saw the angels praising God, saying these same words: "Holy, holy, holy is the LORD of hosts; the whole earth is full of his glory" (Is. 6:3). The Apostle John had a similar experience in the Book of Revelation. When taken up to the worship of God in the heavenly liturgy, he witnessed four living creatures day and night never ceasing to sing, "Holy, holy, holy is the Lord God Almighty" (Rev. 4:8).

hears the mighty voice of a great multitude in heaven singing, "Hallelujah!" and announcing the wedding supper of the Lamb. Jesus Christ, the victorious Lamb of God, has come to wed His Bride, the Church. All throughout salvation history, marriage imagery has been used to describe the intimate union that God wishes to have with His people. In Revelation 19, this intimate covenant communion is finally established in a new Passover feast, with the Lamb, Jesus Christ, uniting Himself to His Bride, the Church. Announcing this wedding banquet, an angel says, "Blessed are those who are invited to the marriage supper of the Lamb" (Rev. 19:9).

Holy Communion of the Bride and Groom

So when the priest at Mass says, "Happy are those who are called to this supper," he is not inviting us to any ordinary meal. He is passing on to us the angelic wedding announcement from the Book of Revelation. At this moment in the Mass, we are being called to the marriage supper of the Lamb. And when we walk up to receive Holy Communion, we are meant to play the role of the most honored Bride! Indeed, our divine Bridegroom unites Himself to us in the most intimate way possible here on earth by giving us His Real Presence, His own Body, Blood, Soul, and Divinity in the Eucharist.

In this light, we can see most clearly that the Mass is no empty ritual or man-made tradition. Rather, it is a participation in the heavenly wedding feast of the Lamb. And all the prayers and rituals of the Mass ultimately are meant to prepare us for this climactic moment of the liturgy. Like a bride who longs to be one with her groom, so our hearts should be filled with ardent longing for Holy Communion with our divine Bridegroom, whose very Eucharistic Body enters into ours in this most profound union. Indeed, we are most blessed to share in this real communion with our God, as the angel in the Book of Revelation so fittingly declares: "Blessed are those who are invited to the marriage supper of the Lamb" (Rev. 19:9).

Edward P. Sri, S.T.D., holds a doctorate from the Angelicum in Rome and is an author or coauthor of several books and articles on Scripture and apologetics, including Mystery of the Kingdom: On the Gospel of Matthew *(Emmaus Road) and* The New Rosary in Scripture: Biblical Insights for Praying the 20 Mysteries *(Charis). He is also a popular speaker on Catholic subjects.*

CHAPTER II

The Mass and the Synoptic Gospels

CURTIS MITCH

Timing, as they say, is everything. The young man with marriage on his mind wouldn't dream of proposing to the woman he loves while he's taking out the garbage or brushing his teeth or engaging in some other completely ordinary activity. No, he racks his brain for weeks in advance, planning how to create that special moment that he hopes will become his happiest memory. If he jumps the gun and pops the question too soon, the whole thing is sure to seem awkward and off balance. Of course, if he waits too long, procrastination could have the same uncharming effect. Everything has to be timed just right.

The Synoptic Gospels make the same point about the Last Supper. Matthew, Mark, and Luke all agree that Jesus timed this event to coincide with the Jewish feast of Passover (Mt. 26:18; Mk. 14:12; Lk. 22:8). There's something remarkable about this when we unroll the story of His life. We know, for instance, that Jesus shared countless meals with friends and admirers throughout His years of ministry. Scene after scene in the Gospels, Jesus dines at table with disciples, scribes, tax collectors, and sinners. With so many opportunities to act, why did Jesus wait until this very last meal to institute the Eucharist and make it the first Mass? What was the point of suspending this messianic moment until the paschal festivities got underway?

The answer is found in the Passover itself, a feast that resonates with themes of redemption, recollection, sacrifice, covenant, and divine love. Jesus made Passover the picture frame of the Last Supper to fill these traditional themes with new meaning and to lift them to a new height of significance and fulfillment. We, therefore, can learn much by studying how Jesus transformed the Jewish Passover into the Christian Mass. We can almost say it this way: if we *don't* understand the paschal setting of the Last Supper, we *won't* understand the full magnificence of the Eucharistic liturgy that springs from it. So let's go back to the texts and traditions of Scripture to gain a new appreciation of this messianic feast.

The Jewish Passover

Quite simply, Passover was a liturgical celebration of the Exodus. It was a time for Israel to gather as a nation and look back on its first experience of salvation. At the heart of the Passover drama is the historic rescue of Israel from bondage and their mass migration out of northern Egypt. The Book of Exodus chronicles this epic adventure and enshrines the Passover tradition.

More than anything, Exodus remembers Yahweh as the divine hero behind Israel's liberation. Moses played his part, of course, but the Lord did the real work of deliverance. When Pharaoh hardened his will in defiance and refused to let Israel go, it was Yahweh who hammered Egypt into submission with ten terrifying plagues (Ex. 7–12). When Egyptian forces overtook the fleeing caravans, it was Yahweh who bared His holy arm and blasted a path of escape through the Red Sea (Ex. 14:1–21). When Pharaoh's chariots raced across the seafloor in daring pursuit, it was Yahweh who slammed down the walls of water with crushing force, burying horse and rider in the depths of the sea (Ex. 14:22–31). And when the families of Israel stood safely on the opposite shore, it was Yahweh they praised as their Defender, Redeemer, and King (Ex. 15:1–18).

Israel's role in this deliverance centered on the Passover meal, called the Seder. Exodus 12:1–27 outlines the shape of this ritual feast: on the evening of the first Passover, families gathered together to sacrifice a lamb, smear its blood on their doorframes, and eat its roasted flesh with unleavened bread and bitter herbs. Each of these elements is imbued with sacred symbolism. The flesh and blood of the lambs were a sign of the Lord's salvation (Ex. 12:13, 26–27); the unleavened bread was a token of the hurried escape from Egypt that lay ahead for Israel (Ex. 12:33–34); and the bitter herbs gave families a final taste of the bitter bondage they were leaving behind (Ex. 1:14; Ex. 12:8; Num. 9:11).

It is vitally important to understand the purpose of the Passover celebration. For the Exodus generation, dutiful observance of the paschal rubrics was a protective shield against the sword of the tenth plague—the death of every firstborn in Egypt (Ex. 12:21–28). For all subsequent generations, the Passover feast was a "memorial," that is, a liturgical mechanism for retrieving the sacred past and pulling it into the present (Ex. 12:14). By performing the ritual actions of the Seder, participants are put in touch with the blessings of the historic Exodus. It enables them to taste and see the salvation of God and join together with the generation that lived through it. In effect, remembrance and recollection are not enough; the goal is to relive the deliverance personally, nationally, and spiritually. A Jewish tract on the Passover puts it this way: "In every generation a man must so regard himself as if he came forth himself out of Egypt."[1]

These are the essential features of the Passover that have remained stable through the centuries. Yet after the time of Moses, the paschal liturgy did undergo development. We know that the Seder in Jesus' day was certainly more elaborate than the one eaten by the Exodus generation.[2] Alongside the traditional lamb, unleavened bread, and bitter herbs, wine was added to the menu to heighten the sense of celebration. Also placed on the table was *haroset*, a pasty mixture of fruits and nuts mashed together with vinegar and cinnamon. Hymns became a

---

[1] Mishnah *Pesahim* 10.5, cited from *The Mishnah*, trans. Herbert Danby, D.D. (London: Oxford University Press, 1933), 151. The Mishnah is a compilation of Palestinian Jewish traditions put in writing about AD 200.

[2] For surveys of the Passover meal in relation to the Last Supper, see Joachim Jeremias, *The Eucharistic Words of Jesus* (London: SCM Press, 1966) and I. Howard Marshall, *Last Supper and Lord's Supper* (Grand Rapids: Wm. B. Eerdmans, 1980). I recommend these works for their historical rather than their theological stance.

regular feature as well: Psalms 113–118, called the Hallel Psalms, filled the atmosphere with praise and thanksgiving. Traces of these elements, both edible and audible, can be found in the Last Supper narratives.[3]

In terms of structure, the Passover Seder, during the time of Jesus, unfolded in four movements or courses. The first movement began with a festal blessing of the day and the passing around of the first cup of wine (the *qiddush* cup). This was followed by a preliminary course of green herbs, bitter herbs, and *haroset*. The second movement included the retelling of the Passover story, the singing of the first Hallel hymn—either Psalm 113 or Psalms 113 and 114 together—and the drinking of the second cup (the *haggadah* cup). The third movement was the heart of the celebration—the main meal. It began with the blessing of unleavened bread and continued with a feast of lamb, unleavened bread, and more bitter herbs. After dinner, participants shared the third cup of wine (the *berakah* cup). The fourth movement ended the festivities with the chanting of the final Hallel Psalms and a blessing over the final cup (the *hallel* cup).

Mindful of this historical and theological background, let us join Jesus at the Last Supper and carefully weigh His words and actions. For it is the Passover setting that gives the institution of the Eucharist some of its richest theological meaning.

---

[3] The Synoptic Gospels mention unleavened bread and at least one cup of wine (Mt. 26:26–27; Mk. 14:22–23; Lk. 22:19–20). *Haroset* is not mentioned directly, but some scholars see a hint of its presence in Jesus' words about dipping in "the dish" (Mt. 26:23; Mk. 14:20). The Hallel Psalms are alluded to in the "hymn" sung after the meal (Mt. 26:30; Mk. 14:26).

This Is My Body

The Last Supper narratives waste no time in getting to the "good part." The evangelists could have detailed the Passover rituals that led up to the Eucharist—what we have outlined above as the first and second movements of the Seder—but they did not.[4] Instead, they bring us straight to the main meal.

The Passover host begins this movement by blessing the unleavened bread. In doing this he was supposed to give a symbolic description of the loaf as "the bread of affliction" (Deut. 16:3). Jesus, however, does something unexpected. He abandons the traditional words of interpretation and replaces them with words of consecration: "Take, eat; this is my body" (Mt. 26:26). The innovation here is stunning, but even more so the mystery. What did Jesus mean? Was He speaking literally, as in, "I'm holding My sacred humanity in My hands, and now I'm giving Myself to you as food"? Or, did He intend His words figuratively, like the man who pulls a picture out of his wallet and says, "This is my wife and kids"?

Strangely enough, linguistic analysis is not very helpful here. Scholars who find a literal meaning unsettling are quick to point out that the verb "is" has a range of possible meanings in Greek. It can express not only identity, but also attribute, cause, resemblance, and fulfillment.[5] And to make matters even more interesting, Jesus must have spoken these words in a Semitic language, which means He never

---

[4] Luke hints at the preliminary phase when he speaks of an earlier cup in Luke 22:17.

[5] For this brand of discussion by Protestant scholars, see G. B. Caird, *The Language and Imagery of the Bible* (Grand Rapids: Wm. B. Eerdmans, 1997), 100–02; and D. A. Carson *Exegetical Fallacies*, 2nd ed. (Grand Rapids: Baker Books, 1996), 57–60.

actually uttered the word "is." Instead He used a verb-less clause of predication ("this, my body") meaning that the verbal element is implied rather than stated. So how can we be sure that the Catholic understanding is correct, namely, that Jesus was speaking literally and sacramentally and not just figuratively or symbolically?

I submit that the Passover context supplies the literal meaning. Recall where we are in the course of the paschal liturgy. This is the main meal, and Passover participants arrive at this summit when they eat the "flesh" of the Seder lamb (Ex. 12:8). But here, the words of consecration reveal that Jesus has just placed *Himself* at the center of the Passover celebration. In effect, He has replaced the traditional lamb and made His own flesh the heart of the feast. It is a curious fact, by the way, that none of the Gospels actually mention the presence of a lamb in the upper room.[6] The omission of this all-important centerpiece of the meal is suggestive, to say the least. It hints that Jesus has deliberately staged a lambless Passover to make the point that *He* is the true Lamb and the true festival food that makes the lambs of the old liturgy no longer necessary or relevant.

In Scripture passages outside the Synoptic Gospels, we have clear confirmation that Jesus is the true Lamb of the Passover meal. In fact, we can show that Jesus had already prepared His disciples to make this connection before celebrating the Last Supper. The

---

[6] Admittedly, some scholars read "this passover" in Luke 22:15 as meaning, "this passover lamb." The argument is less than convincing, however, not least because the very next verse, Luke 22:16, has Jesus vowing not to eat "it" again until all is fulfilled in the kingdom. Are we to think that Jesus is looking forward to one last taste of mutton before the kingdom arrives in glory? No scholar or theologian I know of ventures to make such a claim.

Gospel of John gives us an entire sermon from Jesus,
called the Bread of Life Discourse, that expounds
upon Eucharistic themes (Jn. 6:35–59). According to
the evangelist, it was delivered as the feast of Passover
was drawing near (Jn. 6:4). Here we see Jesus, already
identified as the Lamb of God (Jn. 1:29), driving
home the point with emphatic repetition that "unless
you eat the flesh of the Son of man and drink his
blood, you have no life in you" (Jn. 6:53). What
context, other than the paschal Last Supper, makes
adequate sense of these words? Recall too that
John surrounds Jesus with Passover themes at the
Crucifixion scene. One of the most poignant is when
the soldiers exempt Jesus from the Roman custom of
crushing the legs of the executed victim with a mal-
let (Jn. 19:33). John sees this fulfilling an important
Passover stipulation: "Not a bone of him shall be
broken" (Jn. 19:36). He is referring to the restriction
in Exodus 12:46 that paschal lambs could not incur
skeletal trauma if they were to qualify for the Seder.
The same requirement is now met in Jesus. He dies
as the Eucharistic Lamb with bones intact, implying
that His flesh now qualifies for consumption in the
Church's paschal liturgy.

Paul develops this same thinking in his catechesis
to the Corinthians. He is forthright that Jesus Christ
is "our paschal lamb," who has already been slain
in sacrifice (1 Cor. 5:7). Notice that, for Paul, the
significance of this doesn't end with sacrifice and
death. Rather, it summons us to "celebrate the festival" (1 Cor. 5:8). It calls us to the table of the Lord
where Eucharistic communion is "a participation in
the body of Christ" (1 Cor. 10:16).[7]

---

[7] With more space we could broaden our search by venturing outside the

This Is My Blood

In His next action, Jesus takes and blesses a cup of wine. This is the third cup of the Passover Seder, what is traditionally called the *berakah* or blessing cup. We know this, first, because Luke places it immediately "after supper" (Lk. 22:20), second, because Matthew and Mark follow it up with the singing of the second Hallel "hymn" (Mt. 26:30; Mk. 14:26), and third, because Paul identifies the Eucharistic chalice with the traditional "cup of blessing" (1 Cor. 10:16).

Here again, Jesus follows the Seder ritual and yet departs from it in a significant way. This time He says: "Drink of it, all of you; for this is my blood of the covenant, which is poured out for many for the forgiveness of sins" (Mt. 26:27–28). Now a second mystery stands before us. Besides identifying the festal wine with the lifeblood of His humanity—words that should also be taken literally, just like the blessing over the bread—what did He mean by "blood of the covenant"? Not surprisingly, this too has ties with the saving drama of the Passover.

The words "blood of the covenant" are lifted from a famous line in the Book of Exodus. The scene is the foot of Mount Sinai where the liberated families of Israel have regrouped after their difficult journey out of Egypt. On the mountaintop stands

---

Bible into the historical context of early Christianity. It is absolutely certain, for instance, that the Church Fathers understood the words of consecration literally, judging from the mountain of testimony left behind in their writings. In fact, Christians were so united on this point that the Church felt no need to give an official interpretation of the Eucharistic words until the rise of Protestantism in the sixteenth century (Council of Trent: session 13, chapters 1 and 4). The pronouncements can be found in *Decrees of the Ecumenical Councils*, vol. 2, *Trent to Vatican II*, ed. Norman P. Tanner, S.J. (Washington, DC: Georgetown University Press, 1990), 693–95.

Yahweh in fire and smoke, and glory. At the base stands Moses, who prepares the tribes to enter a covenant of kinship and communion with the Lord. To ratify this new relationship, bulls are offered in sacrifice and their blood is collected in bowls. Half of the blood is dashed on an altar, which represents God, and the other half is splashed on the people. "Behold," Moses says, "the blood of the covenant which the LORD has made with you" (Ex. 24:8). Through this highly symbolic act, in which blood is a sign of shared kinship and life, the freed people of Israel become the covenant family of Yahweh.

That's the very point Jesus wants to convey in the upper room. The Exodus began with freedom, but it doesn't end until the people of Israel become one family with the Lord. And how is this accomplished? By the blood of covenant sacrifice. The link is not lost on Jesus, who envisions His own blood being "poured out" in a vicarious way. In fact, I suspect that because Jesus has the whole Exodus tradition in mind, both the beginning and the end, He intends for us to think of His own sacrifice in connection with the Passover sacrifice in Egypt (Ex. 12:21–23), as well as the blood sacrifice at Sinai (Ex. 24:5–8). His is the paschal blood that saves us from death, as well as the covenant blood that unites us with God. By effecting the remission of sins, the blood of Jesus brings a new redemption from the death and bondage of sin. At the same time, it seals a new and everlasting covenant that makes us children of the Almighty Father.

Do This in Memory of Me

To complete our study, we should point out that the apostle Paul adds a significant detail about the Last Supper—a detail that Matthew and Mark breeze over and Luke mentions only in part (Lk. 22:19). Namely, that after Jesus consecrated the bread, and then again after He consecrated the wine, He said to the apostles at table: "Do this in remembrance of me" (1 Cor. 11:24–25). These trailing words are by no means an afterthought. They mark a shift from the declarative ("This is . . .") to the imperative ("Do this . . .") that builds on the tradition of Passover.

Recall that when Yahweh gave detailed directions for the first Seder, He said, "This day shall be for you a memorial day" (Ex. 12:14). We have already discussed the basic meaning of this: the Passover memorial tries to reach across the centuries and make contact with the saving power of God that burst into history in Moses' day. It was designed, in other words, to make the Exodus experience a yearly experience for each subsequent generation.

Jesus takes this Passover tradition and sets it on a whole new foundation. He, like Yahweh in Egypt, is giving directions for a new liturgy to be celebrated for generations to come. Although modeled in part on the Seder, this new worship will memorialize the saving grace of God that is now beginning to flood into history through the gates of the Last Supper. No longer is the rescue from Egypt the focal point of the paschal meal, but all eyes and hearts are directed to Jesus. Everything is to be done in commemoration of Him. And because He is truly present in the meal, in the fullness of His humanity and divinity, the liturgical celebration of the Mass gives us real and living

contact with the Lamb of God who died for our
salvation.

Christ, Our Paschal Savior

In the end, the Synoptic accounts of the Last
Supper leave us with a unified impression: Jesus
has gathered the apostles into the upper room to
transform an old feast into a completely new one.
In one sense, the Liturgy of the Eucharist succeeds
the ancient liturgy of the Passover. But even more,
it supercedes this memorial meal in every essential
respect. In place of the old lamb, we have the *true
Lamb* made present in the sacrament. In place of the
old Exodus from Egypt, we have a *new Exodus* from
the spiritual pharaohs of sin and death. In place of
the old covenant, we have the *new Covenant* sealed
in the blood of the Savior. In place of the old liturgy,
we have the *new Liturgy* that makes Christ and His
redemption present every time the Mass is celebrated
in His memory.

Let us allow this vision to give life to our hearts
and minds when we celebrate the sacred mysteries
of the Mass. Let us remind ourselves that we are
living with Jesus at the summit of salvation history. And let us sing with the choirs of heaven to our
paschal Savior: "Worthy is the Lamb who was slain,
to receive power and wealth and wisdom and might
and honor and glory and blessing!" (Rev. 5:12).

*Curtis Mitch received his master's degree in theology
from Franciscan University of Steubenville. He is
coauthor of* The Ignatius Catholic Study Bible *and
a regular contributor to the* Catholic for a Reason
series.

CHAPTER III

Come Again?
The Real Presence As Parousia

SCOTT HAHN

There is a world of difference between the way we talk about the Real Presence today and the way the ancient Church talked about the doctrine.

Catholics today often speak of the Real Presence in terms of a crisis—that is, a crisis of faith. In 1992, a Gallup poll concluded that only thirty percent of Catholics in the United States believe that the bread and wine become the Body and Blood of Christ, while "nearly seventy percent . . . hold erroneous beliefs about Christ's presence in the Eucharist."[1] Thus, a large majority would seem to disbelieve, or simply not know, the Church's perennial teaching: "At the heart of the Eucharistic celebration are the bread and wine that, by the word of Christ and the invo-

---

[1] Rev. Frank Chacon and Jim Burnham, introduction to *Beginning Apologetics 3: How to Explain and Defend the Real Presence of Christ in the Eucharist* (Farmington, NM: San Juan Catholic Seminars, 2000), 4.

cation of the Holy Spirit, become Christ's Body and Blood" (*Catechism*, no. 1333).

A 1997 study produced results similar to those of 1994. Since then, bishops, catechists, and even scholars have worried about this data, and pondered how the Church might solve the problem.

The Catechism of the Catholic Church provides an excellent beginning, in a section titled "The presence of Christ by the power of his word and the Holy Spirit" (nos. 1373–1381). The section states the fact of the Real Presence and speaks at some length about the process that converts the elements of bread and wine into Christ's Body and Blood. "This change the holy Catholic Church has fittingly and properly called transubstantiation [Council of Trent (1551): DS 1642; cf. Mt. 26:26 ff.; Mk. 14:22 ff.; Lk. 22:19 ff.; 1 Cor. 11:24 ff.]" (no. 1376). The *Catechism* then moves to the logical conclusion of belief in transubstantiation:[2] adoring worship of the Eucharist.

---

[2] Pope John Paul II in the Encyclical Letter, *Ecclesia de Eucharistia* defines transubstantiation:

> The sacramental re-presentation of Christ's sacrifice, crowned by the resurrection, in the Mass involves a most special presence which—in the words of Paul VI—"is called 'real' not as a way of excluding all other types of presence as if they were 'not real', but because it is a presence in the fullest sense: a substantial presence whereby Christ, the God-Man, is wholly and entirely present". This sets forth once more the perennially valid teaching of the Council of Trent: "the consecration of the bread and wine effects the change of the whole substance of the bread into the substance of the body of Christ our Lord, and of the whole substance of the wine into the substance of his blood. And the holy Catholic Church has fittingly and properly called this change transubstantiation". Truly the Eucharist is a *mysterium fidei*, a mystery which surpasses our understanding and can only be received in faith, as is often brought out in the catechesis of the Church Fathers regarding this divine sacrament: "Do not see—Saint Cyril of Jerusalem exhorts—in the bread and wine merely natural elements, because the Lord has expressly said that they are his body and his blood: faith assures you of this, though your senses suggest otherwise" (*EE* 15).

The word *transubstantiation* is fitting and proper, and the *Catechism*'s description of the process is succinct yet profound. But these are not the ultimate solution to the Church's crisis of Eucharistic faith. For the term describes a process, but not the end result of that process. For that, we need to press on in our study and contemplation. As the *Catechism* itself reminds us: "We do not believe in formulas, but in those realities they express, which faith allows us to touch. 'The believer's act of faith does not terminate in the propositions, but in the realities which they express' [Saint Thomas Aquinas, *STh* II-II, 1, 2 *ad* 2]" (no. 170).

What is the reality expressed by the formula? What, in essence, is the presence that faith allows us to touch?

In this study, I would like to return to the sources of Christian doctrine, Scripture and Tradition, to discover—and recover—the authentic understanding of Jesus' Real Presence. Therein, I believe, lies the resolution of the crisis of Eucharistic faith, and many other crises as well, both personal and communal.

Opening Presence

The early Christians also spoke of the Real Presence in terms of crisis, but a different sort of crisis. They spoke of the Real Presence in the language of *apocalypse*—the Second Coming, the consummation of history, the end of the world. Indeed, in the works of the Church Fathers and in the earliest liturgies, "Eucharist" and "second coming" are often treated as equivalent terms, showing the close link between the two meanings of the "coming" of Christ. The Eucharist is the awaited parousia, the coming of Christ, exactly as Jesus Himself promised it would be, exactly as Saint Paul described it, exactly as Saint John saw it "in the Spirit on the Lord's day" (Rev. 1:10).

The Eucharist is the parousia. I have given many lectures on this subject since 1999, when I published *The Lamb's Supper: The Mass as Heaven on Earth*. In that book, I examined the Book of Revelation in light of the liturgies of the Church and of Israel, and I examined the Church's Mass in light of the biblical Apocalypse. Most of my readers and listeners were aware that the Book of Revelation had something to say about the coming of Jesus at the end of the world. Few knew, however, that the Book of Revelation had anything to say about Jesus' coming in the Eucharist.

The idea seems alien to faithful churchgoers in the twenty-first century. Yet it was commonplace to Christians of the first, second, and third centuries; and, to scholars of history—whether Catholic or not—the notion appears so pervasive as to be obvious. The great historical theologian Jaroslav Pelikan, writing as a Lutheran, observed of the early Church: "The coming of Christ was 'already' and 'not yet': he had come already—in the incarnation, and on the basis of the incarnation would come in the Eucharist; he had come already in the Eucharist, and would come at the last in the new cup that he would drink with them in his Father's kingdom."[3]

Though a final parousia will one day come, the

---

[3] Jaroslav Pelikan, *The Emergence of the Catholic Tradition* (100–600), vol. 1, in *The Christian Tradition: A History of the Development of Doctrine* series (Chicago: University of Chicago Press, 1971), 126. See also Oscar Cullmann, "The Meaning of the Lord's Supper in Primitive Christianity," in *Essays on the Lord's Supper*, in *Ecumenical Studies in Worship* series, no. 1 (London: Lutterworth, 1958), 15: "Hence, in the early Church, the Lord's Supper involved the presence of Christ in its threefold relation with Easter, with the cult and with the *Parousia*."

Eucharist is the parousia here and now. Anglican scholar Gregory Dix wrote that this notion was "universal" by the third century, and probably long before, since he adds that there are no exceptions to this rule: "[N]o pre-Nicene author Eastern or Western whose Eucharistic doctrine is at all fully stated" holds a different view.[4]

Consider just two examples. The ancient Jerusalem liturgy of Saint James announces: "Let all mortal flesh be silent, and stand with fear and trembling, and meditate nothing earthly within itself: for the King of kings and Lord of lords, Christ our God, comes forward."[5] The Egyptian liturgy of Saint Sarapion proclaims: "This sacrifice is full of your glory."[6] Similar passages can be found in the liturgies of Saint Mark, Saint Hippolytus, the Apostolic Constitutions, Saint John Chrysostom, Saint Cyril of Alexandria, as well as the Roman Canon.[7]

What the ancients saw in the liturgy was the coming of Christ, the parousia; and what they meant by parousia is what we today should mean by the Real Presence. But our ancestors seem to have held that belief more firmly, and understood it more fully, than most Catholics do today.

If we want to recover such universality of belief,

---

[4] Gregory Dix, *The Shape of the Liturgy* (London: A&C Black, 1945), 252–53.

[5] "The Cherubic Hymn," in *The Divine Liturgy of Saint James, the Holy Apostle and Brother of the Lord*, sect. II, in *Ante-Nicene Fathers*, vol. 7, eds. Alexander Roberts and James Donaldson (Peabody, MA: Hendrickson, 1994), 540.

[6] John Wordsworth, ed. and trans., *Bishop Sarapion's Prayer-Book: An Egyptian Summary Dated Probably about AD 350–356* (London: Society for Promoting Christian Knowledge, 1899), 61.

[7] For an excellent discussion of these and similar passages, see Jerome Gassner, O.S.B., *The Canon of the Mass*, (New York: Herder, 1950), 158.

we might start again at the beginning. Thus, I propose to revisit a number of relevant biblical texts
and read them with the Church Fathers, to see what
so many people today are missing when they go to
Mass.

Get Real

When I say that we speak differently of the
Real Presence today, I do not mean to imply that
the content of faith has changed. It hasn't. In fact,
the *Catechism of the Catholic Church* presents
much of its Eucharistic doctrine in quotations from
Church Fathers who lived before the year 200. The
Catechism echoes the flesh-and-blood realism of
the earliest Christians when it says: "[T]he bread
and wine . . . become Christ's Body and Blood" (no.
1333).

To say this is to take Jesus Christ at His word:
"This is my body" (Lk. 22:19), He pronounced over
the bread at the Last Supper. And He preached at
the synagogue of Capernaum: "I am the living bread
which came down from heaven; if any one eats of this
bread, he will live for ever; and the bread which I shall
give for the life of the world is my flesh" (Jn. 6:51).

What did these statements mean to the early
Church? In the year 107, Saint Ignatius of Antioch
said that it was a mark of true faith to confess the
Eucharist "to be the flesh of our Savior Jesus Christ,
which suffered for our sins, and which the Father,
in His goodness, raised up again."[8] Some fifty years
later, Saint Justin Martyr wrote that "the food bless-

---

[8] Saint Ignatius of Antioch, *Epistle of Ignatius to the Smyrneans*, chap.
VII, in *Ante-Nicene Fathers*, vol. 1, eds. Alexander Roberts and James
Donaldson (Peabody, MA: Hendrickson, 1994), 89.

ed by the prayer of His word . . . is the flesh and blood of Jesus who was made flesh."[9]

"Bread and wine" become "Body and Blood." The Church took Christ at His word. This doctrine faced no significant challenge in the first Christian millennium. In every generation and in every geographic corner of the Church, the Fathers bore witness to the Real Presence: Irenaeus of Lyons, Hippolytus of Rome, Tertullian of Carthage, Clement of Alexandria, Cyril of Jerusalem, John Chrysostom of Antioch. Even Theodore of Mopsuestia, a man whose christology of "indwelling" was condemned as heretical, could not bring himself to speak of the Eucharist in any but the realistic and sacramental terms of the Church—even though that realism was incompatible with his own theological method.[10]

The early Christians spoke with one voice in this matter. Yet they did not speak at length, for they observed a certain discretion, which today we call the "discipline of the secret." The sacraments were most sacred—they were actions of the Lord Himself—and so they were not to be publicly disputed, scientifically probed, or otherwise subjected to unnecessary scrutiny.

Since no one disputed the doctrine, philosophical theology had little to say about the Real Presence until the turn of the second millennium. Only then did heresies arise to challenge the doctrine; only then did theologians develop a technical vocabulary, in order to refute the heresies.

[9] Saint Justin Martyr, *The First Apology of Justin*, as quoted in Mike Aquilina, *The Mass of the Early Christians* (Huntington, IN: Our Sunday Visitor, 2001), 41.
[10] Cf. Pelikan, *The Christian Tradition*, 236–37.

Paul in Person

But it is not the specialized vocabulary that I want to examine here. Those terms are helpful, but they are secondary. In this brief space, I wish instead to look at what is primary.

Thus, it is to the Bible I want to return, to certain inspired words about Jesus' Real Presence.

It is easy enough to see where in Scripture the Fathers learned their flesh-and-blood realism. Christ's Eucharistic words are plain enough, in the sixth chapter of John's Gospel and in the four accounts of the Last Supper (cf. Mt. 26:27–29; Mk. 14:22–25; Lk. 22:14–20; 1 Cor. 11:23–26). But where in the New Testament did they find their Eucharistic understanding of the parousia—which seems so unlike the modern ideas of both the Real Presence and the Second Coming?

The Greek word *parousia* means "coming, arrival, or advent." In Christian parlance, it has come to mean, specifically, Christ's return in glory at the end of time. Jesus Himself used the term many times in describing this eschatological event. For example: "as the lightning comes from the east and shines as far as the west, so will be the coming [parousia] of the Son of man" (Mt. 24:27).

Because of such passages, it can be difficult for us to think of parousia as meaning anything but a "coming in glory"—a dramatic divine interruption of history. But that is a theological projection onto a fairly common, and even mundane, Greek word. "Coming in glory" was not the meaning of the word in its original usage. Parousia could describe the visit of an emperor or king, and it was sometimes used that way. It could also describe a much less impressive event.

When Saint Paul, for example, speaks of his own parousia, he gives it a decidedly self-deprecating cast: "For they [Paul's critics] say, 'His letters are weighty and strong, but his bodily presence [parousia] is weak, and his speech of no account'" (2 Cor. 10:10).

Note that, here, all Paul means by his own parousia is his "bodily presence," which he insists is unimpressive to the senses. He uses the word in the same sense in his letter to the Philippians: "Therefore, my beloved, as you have always obeyed, so now, not only as in my presence [parousia] but much more in my absence, work out your own salvation with fear and trembling" (Phil. 2:12).

In both passages, Paul uses parousia to mean an immediate bodily presence, a presence that is real, though visually and aurally unimposing.

Is it not likely that Jesus used the word parousia to connote the same things? Is it not possible that He meant a bodily presence that was real, but unimposing to the senses?

I acknowledge that this is not the interpretation of parousia given by many modern preachers, especially among evangelical and fundamentalist Protestants. But consider the expectations of Jesus' own generation. The Jews of His time read the Old Testament prophecies as predictions of a messiah who would come with military power, overwhelming his enemies with spectacular victories. They were not prepared for a carpenter who laid down His life as a victim.

Instant Gratification

Jesus had promised repeatedly that the kingdom was coming without delay. Midway through the "little apocalypse" of Matthew's Gospel, Jesus says:

"Truly, I say to you, this generation will not pass away till all these things take place" (Mt. 24:35).

The early Christians expected immediate fulfillment of Jesus' prophecies. They expected an imminent parousia. Modern historians have found evidence of this expectation throughout the New Testament and the earliest Christian writings. The most ancient Eucharistic prayer that has survived, in the *Didache*, ends with the Aramaic word *"Maranatha,"* that is, "Come, Lord!" The Book of Revelation begins with a promise to show "what must soon take place" (Rev. 1:1) and ends with the same words as the liturgy in the *Didache*: "Come, Lord Jesus!" Biblical scholar Margaret Barker has identified this word—*"Maranatha!"*—as the Church's primal Eucharistic prayer: "This links the return of the LORD to the Eucharist. Other lines of the [*Didache's*] prayer are ambiguous: 'Let this present world pass away', for example, could imply either a literal understanding of the LORD's return or the present transforming effect of the Eucharist. Maranatha in the Eucharist, however, must be the original epiklesis, praying for the coming of the LORD."[11]

Modern historians are right to point out the expectation of the apostolic age. They go wrong, however, when they conclude that the early Christians must have been disappointed with the passing of time. The apostate scholar Alfred Loisy observed that Jesus came promising the kingdom, but all He left behind was the Church. Loisy was disappointed by this turn of events, but the early Christians most certainly were not.

The early Christians knew that there would indeed be a parousia at the end of time, but there was no less

---

[11] Margaret Barker, "Excursus: *Parousia* and the Liturgy," in *The Revelation of Jesus Christ* (Edinburgh: T&T Clark, 2000), 373.

a parousia right now, whenever they celebrated the Mass. When Christ comes at the end of time, He will have no less glory than He has whenever He comes to His Church in the Mass. The only difference, then, is in what we see.

Faced with the evidence of the ancient liturgies, skeptics will sometimes resort to psychoanalyzing the ancients. They say that the idea of a "liturgical *parousia*" was a late development and a coping mechanism for a disappointed Church. But it wasn't late. Gregory Dix notes that it is in the very earliest documents; indeed, some scholars estimate that the liturgy of the *Didache* could have been written no later than AD 48.[12] After reviewing all the ancient Eucharistic texts, Jaroslav Pelikan concludes: "The Eucharistic liturgy was not a compensation for the postponement of the *parousia*, but a way of celebrating the presence of one who had promised to return."[13]

After all, it was Jesus Himself who set such a high level of expectation in the Church; and it was Jesus Himself who pointed to its imminent fulfillment. Indeed, it was Jesus who established the Eucharist as an eschatological event—a parousia—a coming of the King and the kingdom. We must not miss the small but significant details in the scriptural accounts of the Last Supper. As Jesus takes the bread and wine, He says to His apostles: "I have earnestly desired to eat this passover with you before I suffer; for I tell you I shall not eat it until it is fulfilled in the kingdom of God. . . . I shall not drink of the fruit of the vine

---

[12] On the dating of the *Didache*, see Enrico Mazza, *The Origins of Eucharistic Prayer* (Collegeville, MN: The Liturgical Press, 1995), 40–41.

[13] Pelikan, *The Christian Tradition*, 126–27, italics in original.

until the kingdom of God comes" (Lk. 22:15–16, 18). As He institutes the sacrament, He institutes the kingdom. A moment later, He is speaking of the kingdom in terms of a "table" (22:27) and a "banquet" (22:30)—language that will recur in the final chapters of the Book of Revelation. If we are looking for familiar apocalyptic language, we will find it aplenty in Luke's account of the Last Supper—but we will find it always expressed in Eucharistic terms. Thus, Jesus, using language which calls to mind the Eucharistic element, goes on to speak of apocalyptic trials, in which believers are "sift[ed] like wheat" (22:31).

No less an authority than Joseph Cardinal Ratzinger has noted that the New Testament's apocalyptic imagery is overwhelmingly liturgical, and the Church's liturgical language is overwhelmingly apocalyptic. "The parousia is the highest intensification and fulfillment of the liturgy," he writes. "And the liturgy is parousia. . . . Every Eucharist is parousia, the Lord's coming, and yet the Eucharist is even more truly the tensed yearning that He would reveal His hidden Glory."[14]

Thy Kingdom Come!

None of this precludes a parousia of Christ at the end of history. Theologians call that "coming" of Christ the "plenary parousia"—not because Christ will have a greater fullness then, but rather because we will be able to behold Him in His fullness, with our senses unveiled. For, since His coming, Christ is present in the world in a way that He was

[14] Joseph Cardinal Ratzinger, *Eschatology* (Washington, DC: Catholic University of America Press, 1988), 201, italics omitted.

not in the Old Covenant; but He remains veiled in a way that He will not be at the end. The *Catechism* tells us: "The Kingdom of God has been coming since the Last Supper and, in the Eucharist, it is in our midst. The kingdom will come in glory when Christ hands it over to His Father" (no. 2816).

It is interesting to note that the New Testament speaks not of Christ's "return" but of His "coming." In His Incarnation, He came; and, as He passed from human sight, He promised to sustain His presence forever: "I am with you always, to the close of the age" (Mt. 28:20).

Thus, His parousia—His presence—remains with us, even as we pray for its plenitude. In the same way, we live even now in Christ's kingdom, even though we daily pray, "Thy kingdom come." Contrary to Alfred Loisy's retort, Jesus delivered exactly the kingdom He had promised, and He delivered it as the Church. Recall that our Lord compared the kingdom to a dragnet filled with fish and with trash; recall that He compared it to a field full of both weeds and wheat. He could not have been speaking of the fulfillment of the kingdom at the end of time; for then there will be no trash, no weeds, no tears, no mourning, no crying, no pain, nor anything accursed (cf. Rev. 21:4, 22:3). He was speaking about the Church that we know today—the Church that is the kingdom, the kingdom where the King reigns in the Eucharist.

The kingdom is here now, though we do not yet have eyes to see its fullness. Today we know tears and mourning, but in the Mass, we still pray with the words that Christians used in the liturgy of the *Didache*: "For the kingdom, the power, and the glory are Yours, now and forever."

The *Catechism* sums it up: "The Church knows
that the Lord comes even now in his Eucharist and
that he is there in our midst. However, his presence
is veiled" (no. 1404).

Judgment Day

The Eucharist is the parousia—the Real Presence.
That is the Church's infallible reflection on the scriptural texts. But what difference should this make to
us who go to Mass? The *Catechism* works out the
implications for Christian belief and behavior (cf.
nos. 1373–1378). I commend those points to your
attention; but I would have you read them in light of
Saint Paul's inspired words on the same subject.

To the Christians at Corinth, Paul poses a rhetori-
cal question: "The cup of blessing which we bless, is it
not a participation in the blood of Christ? The bread
which we break, is it not a participation in the body
of Christ?" (1 Cor. 10:16). The word translated as
"participation" is the Greek *koinonia*, which means
"communion" or "sharing." It has the same root as the
word Saint Peter uses when he describes us Christians
as "partakers of the divine nature" (2 Pet. 1:4).

As if to emphasize the reality of this presence, Paul
goes on, several lines later, to tell the story of Jesus'
institution of the Eucharist at the Last Supper, replete
with the words: "This is my body. . . . This cup is
the covenant in my blood" (cf. 1 Cor. 11:23–25).
Quoting Jesus Himself, Paul leaves no doubt as to the
substantial change that takes place in this supreme act
of Christian worship.

Then, once Paul has established this presence, he
evokes the parousia: "For as often as you eat this bread
and drink this cup, you proclaim the Lord's death until

he comes" (v. 26). This resonates with everything else we have learned of the first generation of Christians. In their liturgy, they prayed *"Maranatha!"*—"Come, Lord!"—for they were engaged in the liturgy of His coming, His presence, His parousia.

Lest anyone doubt the reality of this presence— lest anyone think that Christ's Eucharistic presence is somehow lacking in "power and glory"—Paul issues a grave and remarkable warning: "Whoever, therefore, eats the bread or drinks the cup of the Lord in an unworthy manner will be guilty of profaning the body and blood of the Lord. . . . For any one who eats and drinks without discerning the body eats and drinks judgment upon himself" (1 Cor. 11:27, 29).

Whenever the New Testament speaks of Christ's coming, it speaks also of His judgment. The Eucharistic parousia is a real presence—Christ coming in power to judge. His power is evident in its effects on those who receive Communion. Paul speaks specifically of those who receive unworthily and so bring judgment upon themselves. "That is why many of you are weak and ill, and some have died" (1 Cor. 11:30). For such unrepentant sinners, the Eucharist is the final coming of Christ; it is the last judgment.

There is, however, an unspoken corollary to Paul's account of the judgment of sinners. With the Eucharistic parousia comes also the judgment of the saints. If Christ's coming means sickness and death to sinners, how much more will His coming mean blessings and health to those who "discern the Lord's body"?

A liturgy of ancient Egypt expressed this well

at the very moment of consecration, when it asks God to make every communicant worthy "to receive a medicine of life for the healing of every sickness and . . . not for condemnation."[15]

This echoes the still-older praise of Saint Ignatius of Antioch, who called the Eucharist the "medicine of immortality, the antidote against death."[16]

It is the glorified Christ who comes in the Eucharist, for communion with those who are worthy to receive the gift. For the saints, the judgment of the parousia is everlasting life, a share in Christ's own resurrected flesh (cf. *EE* 18). At the end of the second century, Saint Irenaeus could ask: "How can they say that the flesh, which is nourished with the body of the Lord and with his blood, goes to corruption? . . . For the bread, which is produced from the earth, is no longer common bread, once it has received the invocation of God; it is then the Eucharist, consisting of two realities, earthly and heavenly. So also our bodies, when they receive the Eucharist, are no longer corruptible, but have the hope of the resurrection to eternity."[17]

Closer Than You Think

Just before beginning the "little apocalypse" of Matthew's Gospel, Jesus laments over Jerusalem: "Behold, your house is forsaken and desolate. For

---

[15] Wordsworth, *Bishop Sarapion's Prayer-Book*, 63.

[16] Saint Ignatius of Antioch, *Letter to the Ephesians*, in *Ancient Christian Writers, Vol. 1: The Epistles of Saint Clement of Rome and Saint Ignatius of Antioch*, trans. James A. Kleist, S.J. (New York: Newman Press, 1946), 68.

[17] Saint Irenaeus of Lyons, *Against the Heresies*, as quoted in Mike Aquilina, *The Mass of the Early Christians* (Huntington, IN: Our Sunday Visitor, 2001), 92.

I tell you, you will not see me again, until you say, 'Blessed is he who comes in the name of the Lord'" (Mt. 23:38–39).

The citizens of Jerusalem did not discern the body and blood of our Lord when He came, and so they brought judgment upon themselves. This is a sobering thought for a generation that faces a "crisis" in faith in the Real Presence.

Yet the crisis is not necessarily the one that's reflected in survey data. It's a crisis we must all face. Saint Paul's words should remind us that our generation, and every generation, must face the same choice between blessing and judgment, whenever we present ourselves for Holy Communion.

Our Lord promised: "You will not see Me again, until you say, 'Blessed is he who comes in the name of the Lord'"—that is, until the parousia. How right it is for the Church to place those words, "Blessed is he who comes in the name of the Lord," on our lips just moments before the Eucharistic consecration in the Mass, just moments before our Lord's Eucharistic parousia.

If our generation does lack faith in the Eucharist, I think we would profit most from a recovery of the biblical teaching on the sacrament and on the parousia, especially as it is reflected in the *Catechism*.

As Catholics, we must dare to take Jesus at His word and accept His promises on His terms. He promised us a glorious kingdom within His own generation—and, even today, we boldly proclaim that He made good on that promise. For all time, He has established His Eucharistic kingdom, the Church.

What Jesus promised and what He delivered are one and the same. He said He was coming soon—

and He is! He said the kingdom is near—and it is.
It's as near as your local parish, where the King
reigns in the Eucharist. O come, let us adore Him!

*Scott Hahn, Ph.D., an internationally renowned
Catholic lecturer and author, is professor of Scripture and
theology at the Franciscan University of Steubenville
and holds the Cardinal Laghi Chair at the Pontifical
College Josephinum. Dr. Hahn is also founder and
President of the St. Paul Center for Biblical Theology
(http://www.salvationhistory.com). His books include*
Scripture Matters *(Emmaus Road),* Understanding
"Our Father" *(Emmaus Road),* Rome Sweet Home
(Ignatius), The Lamb's Supper *(Doubleday),* Hail Holy
Queen *(Doubleday),* First Comes Love *(Doubleday),*
Lord Have Mercy *(Doubleday),* A Father Who Keeps
His Promises *(Servant).*

CHAPTER IV

He Died Once, but His Sacrifice Lives On
The Mass as Sacrifice

THOMAS NASH

The Catholic Church teaches that Jesus Christ died and offered Himself once for all (Heb. 7:28), yet enables His Church to continue offering that same sacrifice at every Mass.

How can these two apparently conflicting realities be reconciled?

Scripture teaches that Jesus "holds his priesthood permanently" (Heb. 7:24) and primarily exercises it in heaven, for the heavenly sanctuary is where Christ's sacrifice culminated in glory (cf. Heb. 9:23–24). And what is the principle mission of a priest? As Scripture makes clear, Jesus does not intercede for us in heaven in some nebulous way, but by making an offering: "For every high priest is appointed to offer gifts and sacrifices; *hence it is necessary for this priest also to have something to offer*" (Heb. 8:3; emphasis added). Consequently, if Jesus has offered only one sacrifice, and yet holds His priesthood permanently, we can logically conclude that Jesus' sacrifice has a perpetual or everlasting quality, that is, He continues to offer it in heaven. And, while His priestly base is in heaven, not earth (cf. Heb. 8:4), Jesus empowers the Church to continue offering His one sacrifice, allowing His kingdom to come on earth through the ministry of His priests.

Indeed, Christ's one sacrifice and His re-presentation of it in the Mass is a profound mystery. And the key to understanding this mystery can be stated simply: the sacrifice that Jesus commenced on Calvary two thousand years ago did not end on Calvary. All Christians agree that Jesus is a high priest, and that He was both priest and victim in offering Himself on Calvary. In the Old Covenant, when making a sin offering, priests would "pour out" the blood of the victim at the base of the altar (cf. Lev. 4:1–7; 8:14–15). Similarly, in atonement for our sins, Jesus announces at the Last Supper that He will "pour out" His blood to establish a "new covenant in [His] blood" (Lk. 22:20; cf. Mt. 26:28).

But what about subsequent to Calvary, after Jesus poured out His blood? Many Christians argue that what Jesus began on Calvary ended there. They agree with Catholics that Christ's sacrifice has impact far beyond Calvary and that He continues to intercede for us in some way in heaven. But they also argue that the essential sacrificial action that He set out to accomplish started and culminated on Calvary. After all, they contend, Jesus' last words on the Cross were, "It is finished" (Jn. 19:30).

Protestant apologists argue that the Bible never uses the word priest—"*kohen*" (Hebrew) and "*hiereus*" (Greek)—to refer to anyone but Old Covenant priests and Jesus Himself.[1] If Jesus really established New Covenant priests in addition to Himself, why is the term not applied even to His apostles?[2] The Bible speaks of the common priesthood of the faithful (1 Pet. 2:9), but in terms of offering sacrifices—i.e., a ministerial priesthood—the apostles and others are not called priests.[3] While we don't know for sure why the Bible never explicitly refers to the apostles and others as New Covenant priests, Scripture elsewhere makes clear that the leaders in the earthly Church performed the quintessential priestly ministry: offering sacrifices (cf. 1 Cor. 10:14–22, in light of Heb. 8:3).

Setting the Sacrificial Table

There is no question that the first Christians believed they had concrete access to Christ's sacrifice. They understood the Mass as the fulfillment of the Passover sacrifice. Jesus offered the Last Supper in a Passover context (cf. Lk. 22:7–38) and told His apostles to continue His ritualistic actions in memory of Him. Our Lord's words resonated with the first Christians, for, as Jews, they knew that the Passover sacrifice was to be celebrated again and again, that is, as "an ordinance for ever" (Ex. 12:14, 17, 24), which involved not only offering lambs to God but also eating those lambs (cf. Ex. 12:5–9). They also recognized Jesus as superior to the traditional Passover

---

[1] Jesus does not explicitly refer to Himself as a priest, but the Letter to the Hebrews, for example, does.

[2] The biblical term "presbyter," which translates as "elders," eventually became exclusively identified with those who served as New Covenant priests.

[3] One exception is Romans 15:16 where Saint Paul, in discussing his ministering to the Gentiles in the "priestly service of the gospel of God," uses the adjectival form (priestly) of *hiereus* (*hierouogounta*).

lambs, the offering of which had helped deliver Israel
from human bondage in Egypt. They realized that
Jesus is "*the* Lamb of God," whose self-offering "*takes
away the sin of the world*" (Jn. 1:29, emphasis added).
Thus, the first Christians could, with their brother
Saint Paul, affirm that "Christ, our paschal lamb, has
been sacrificed" (1 Cor. 5:7).

And yet, along with Saint Paul, these same first
Christians believed that Christ's sacrifice continued.
In celebrating the memorial of Christ's sacrifice, Paul
teaches that Christians do not partake of ordinary
bread and wine. Rather, the Communion bread is a
partaking of Christ's body and the Communion cup
a partaking of His blood (1 Cor. 10:14–17). After
matter-of-factly affirming Christ's Real Presence in the
Eucharist, Paul indicates how we can eat Christ's flesh
and drink His blood: this New Covenant celebration
makes present His definitive Passover sacrifice. Most
Protestant apologists counter that "the Lord's supper"
(1 Cor. 11:20) is only a symbolic recalling of the Last
Supper, not a sacrificial re-presentation, because Paul
tells the Corinthians that they should not partake of
both the "table" (Greek: *trapeza*) of demons and that
of the Lord (1 Cor. 10:21). If Paul had wanted to convey that the Eucharist is actually a sacrifice, they argue,
he would have instead used the Greek word for "altar,"
i.e., "place of sacrifice" (*thusiasterion*),[4] which he uses
in reference to Israel's altar of sacrifice in the Temple
(1 Cor. 10:18).

---

[4] Paul R. McReynolds, ed., *Word Study Greek-English New Testament*
(Wheaton, IL: Tyndale House, 1998), 619, 818. See also Spiros
Zodhiates, ed., *The Hebrew-Greek Key Study Bible—New American
Standard Bible* (Chattanooga, TN: AMG, 1990), p. 72 (no. 5132) and
p. 37 (no. 2379), respectively, of the "Greek Dictionary of the New
Testament" appendix.

Biblical context, though, is crucial. "Table" (*trape-za*) can mean "altar" if the context is clearly a sacrificial one. Paul makes it unmistakably clear in his analogy that he is talking about eating things that have been sacrificed. As noted, he speaks of Israel's altar of sacrifice in the Temple: "[A]re not those who eat the *sacrifices* partners in the *altar*?" (1 Cor. 10:18, emphasis added). Paul is making reference to the Temple's bronze altar of sacrifice. The prophet Malachi refers to this same sacrificial altar as the "the LORD's table" (Mal. 1:7, 12). One should not therefore presume a non-sacrificial meaning regarding the New Covenant "table of the Lord"(1 Cor. 10:21) just because Paul does not use *thusiasterion*. In discussing the Old Covenant altar of sacrifice located in the Temple, Malachi interchangeably refers to this altar as both an "altar" (Mal. 1:7, 10) *and* the "the LORD's table" (Mal. 1:7, 12). Again, context is crucial.

Consider further that Paul notes that the Corinthians will become "partners with demons" (1 Cor. 10:20)—entering into communion with the henchmen of the devil, the mystical body of Satan—if they eat something that has been offered to idols. To sacrifice to an idol and partake of the sacrifice, Paul says, is necessarily to serve Satan, because the true object of devotion behind every stone or metal idol is the devil who inspired its construction. Paul adds that Christians should consequently not provoke God (1 Cor. 10:22), alluding to the judgment ancient Israel endured when it provoked Yahweh with its own idolatrous practices (Deut. 32:15–38).

Had Paul wanted to distinguish between the actual sacrifices offered in the Temple and those offered to demons on one hand, and a merely symbolic meal of the Eucharist on the other, he would have made a clearer distinction. He would have made sure that the Corinthians did not misunderstand his sacrificial analogy as meaning that the Eucharist *is* a genuine sacrifice. Instead, Paul teaches in a quite contrary manner. First, he emphasizes that the Eucharist is the body and blood of Jesus (1 Cor. 10:14–17) and then, as a logical extension, compares the sacrificial nature of the Eucharist with other contemporary sacrificial meals. He dwells on the peril of partaking of demonic sacrifices, not on clarifying alleged sacrificial misunderstandings about the Eucharist.

Finally, consider another place in which *thusiasterion* is used in the New Testament: "We have an altar (*thusiasterion*) from which those who serve the tent have no right to eat" (Heb. 13:10). The author makes a clear distinction between Old Covenant Temple sacrifices and the sacrifice offered in the New Covenant. Christians have a *thusiasterion*, a real altar on which they not only offer sacrifice, but also partake of that which is offered, the Eucharist. On the other hand, Temple priests and other Jews who cling exclusively to Old Covenant worship may not partake of the Eucharist. This passage provides further evidence that the Mass is the fulfilled, New Covenant Passover. When considered in light of other Eucharistic passages in the New Testament, a merely symbolic reading of Hebrews 13:10 cannot be sustained.

Still the One

Having established the sacrificial nature of the Mass, we consider in more detail another important issue: how could Christ's sacrifice have been offered once for all, two thousand years ago, yet still be offered today?

The answer lies in understanding how sacrifices are offered to God in general, and how Jesus offered His sacrifice in particular. In the Old Testament, there were several types of sacrifice. Those that involved the slaughter of a live victim shared two distinct, yet interdependent phases. That is, you couldn't have an authentic sacrifice without completing both phases. The priest, who served as God's designated mediator for the people, would first *sacrifice* a victim, i.e., deliver over a victim to God by slaughtering it. Second, the priest, on behalf of the people, would *offer* the sacrifice, making contact with God and mediating relations with Him. For example, the priest would touch the victim's blood to the altar, which represented God, or he would send the sacrificial aroma of a victim's burnt body heavenward as "a pleasing odor" to God (cf. Lev. 1:3–10).

To more fully explain the twofold phases of biblical sacrifices that involved the slaughter of victims, let us look at the sacrifices offered on the Day of Atonement (*Yom Kippur*). These are the best examples from the Old Testament in general and the Old Covenant made with Moses in particular. As the Letter to the Hebrews teaches, these sacrifices both prefigured and were perfected by Christ's once-for-all sacrifice of Himself.

Once a year on the Day of Atonement, as described in Leviticus 16:1–34, the high priest of Israel would offer special sacrifices. In particular, he would slaughter and offer a bull to atone for his sins and a goat for those of the nation. To do so, he would enter

the tabernacle or "tent of meeting," which consisted
of three main sections:

—an outer court or courtyard (Ex. 27: 9 ff.);
—an inner court known as the holy place or "holies,"
  (Ex. 26:33); which featured the altar of incense;
  and
—an innermost room known as the most holy place or
  "holy of holies" (26:34), which was separated from
  the holy place by a veil (Ex. 26:33).[5]

The two sacrificial phases of these Day of Atonement
offerings took place in the courtyard and the most
holy place, respectively. The courtyard featured the
altar of sacrifice, the place on which animals were
slaughtered. It was an altar overlaid with bronze and
also known as the altar of burnt offering (Ex. 40:29).
Meanwhile, the most holy place was aptly named, for
there God provided His most intimate presence on
earth. Flanked by two angels, Yahweh was present
upon His mercy seat, which was fixed atop the sacred
Ark of the Covenant (Ex. 25:8, 17–22).

So holy was the most holy place that no one
entered it except the high priest, and he only once a
year on the Day of Atonement. Any other attempt to
enter the most holy place would result in death (Lev.
16:1–2; cf. Num. 3:10, 18:7). In atoning for the sins
of Israel and of the high priest, the Day of Atonement
sacrifices did not begin and end with the slaughter
of the bull and goat on the altar of sacrifice in the
courtyard. To *complete* the sacrifices, the high
priest had to enter the most holy place to offer the
sacrificial victims to God, making atonement for

---

[5] The tabernacle eventually gave way to the much more ornate Temple,
   which also had three similar sections.

Israel's sins by sprinkling their blood in front of and on His mercy seat (Lev. 16:14–15).

Now consider Christ's sacrifice of Calvary. As with the original Day of Atonement sacrifices, the sacrifice of Calvary does not begin and end with Jesus' suffering and death on the Cross on Good Friday, nor even with His Resurrection on Easter Sunday. Rather, Jesus had to enter the heavenly holy place[6] and offer Himself, His own glorified blood, to the Father (Heb. 9:11–12, 23–28). In short, without His Ascension and associated self-offering in the heavenly sanctuary (cf. Jn. 20:17), there would be no fulfillment of the Day of Atonement sacrifices and the Old Covenant, and no completion of His sacrifice begun on Calvary:

> But when Christ appeared as a high priest of the good things that have come, . . . he entered once for all into the Holy Place, taking not the blood of goats and calves[7] but his own blood, thus securing an eternal redemption. . . . For Christ has entered, not into a sanctuary made with hands, a copy of the true one, but into heaven itself, now to appear in the presence of God on our behalf. Nor was it to offer himself repeatedly, as the high priest enters the Holy Place yearly with blood not his own; for then he would have to suffer repeatedly since the foundation of the world. But as it is, he has appeared once for all at the end of the age to put away sin by the sacrifice of himself. (Heb. 9:11, 12, 24–26)

---

[6] The most holy place, also known as "the holy of holies," is sometimes referred to as "the holy place," but with the clear stipulation that this is the holy place *within* the veil, as opposed to the holy place *outside* the veil (compare Ex. 26:33–35 with Lev. 16:11–19 and Heb. 9:11–25). Of course, in the heavenly sanctuary (Heb. 9:12), there can be no veiled barriers between God and man, only a most holy place where the saints dwell face to face with God (cf. 1 Cor. 12:8–12).

[7] "Calves" is a reference to the young bulls offered year after year on the Day of Atonement.

In summary, without Christ's Ascension and His associated Offering in the heavenly sanctuary, there would be no fulfillment of the Day of Atonement sacrifices and the Old Covenant, and no completion of the sacrifice begun on Calvary. While there was never any doubt that the divine Christ would complete the mission His Father gave Him, we need to make proper sacrificial distinctions. When Christ says, "It is finished," (Jn. 19:30), He refers to the earthly phase of His sacrifice, specifically the suffering He endured to atone for our sins. Similarly, when the author of Hebrews says Christ does not "offer himself repeatedly," he refers only to Christ's being slaughtered again and thus "suffering repeatedly" (Heb. 9:25–26). At His Ascension, Jesus commences the heavenly and everlasting phase of His sacrifice. Our Lord enters not into the earthly Temple, but into the heavenly Holy Place before the heavenly mercy seat, making intercession on our behalf before His Father and Our God. Jesus has achieved an "eternal redemption" so there is no need to suffer again.

As noted earlier, because Jesus holds His priesthood permanently, there must be a way for Him to continue offering His once-for-all sacrifice. The earthly, historical aspects (suffering, death, Resurrection) are completed—events never to be repeated. However, the heavenly aspect of His sacrifice, which encompasses and completes what He did on the Cross, never ends—thus the image of the slain Lamb standing triumphantly in heaven (cf. Rev. 5:6, 11–4). Unlike the Old Covenant Day of Atonement, in which the priest would enter and depart from the sanctuary every year, Jesus entered the *heavenly* sanctuary at the Ascension once for all, yet He *remains* to continue ministering as a priest.[8]

We can speak of Christ's heavenly sacrifice as "Calvary completed," for the Mass does not re-crucify Christ. Rather, the Mass makes present the completed, glorified sacrifice of Christ that He forever offers to the Father in heaven. While His glorified Body and Blood are offered at Mass, the earthly aspect of shedding His Blood is not repeated, and thus at each Mass, as the Council of Trent teaches, "the same Christ who offered himself once in a bloody manner on the altar of the cross is contained and offered in an unbloody manner [*Doctrina de ss. Missae sacrificio*, c.2: DS 1743; cf. Heb. 9:14,27]" (*Catechism*, no. 1367).

Realizing that the sacrifice of Calvary has two distinct, yet inseparable phases[9]—including a heavenly, everlasting one—helps us better understand how the Mass can be re-offered or re-presented time and again. The Church sees the Mass as fulfilling the words of the prophet Malachi: "For from the rising of the sun to its setting my name is great among the nations, and in every place incense is offered to my name, and a pure offering; for my name is great among the nations . . . says the LORD of hosts" (Mal. 1:11; cf. *Catechism*, nos. 1350, 2643; 1 Cor. 5:7–8). Indeed, what other, truly pure sacrifice can Christians offer throughout the world on a daily basis?

---

[8] Jesus' self-offering to the Father on our behalf is everlasting, although his intercession for our salvation will culminate at His Second Coming and the Last Judgment.

[9] As noted, the Resurrection can be considered part of the earthly phase of Christ's Sacrifice, but also as a unique, distinct aspect, since only with His Sacrifice is there a Resurrection between the two traditional sacrificial aspects of first slaughtering the victim and then completing the offering of it to God.

That Was Then, This Is Now (and Forever!)

In enabling the re-presentation of His sacrifice at Mass, Christ fulfills the Passover as a "memorial" or "remembrance" (cf. Ex. 12:14). For the ancient Hebrews, remembering was never simply a commemoration of a past event. Rather, when the Hebrews remembered an event, God enabled that event to transcend time and impact the present. The Passover would always remain a limited, past event, for Moses, Pharaoh, and all the others lived out the Passover in a specific time and place. Their actions began and ended that day. And each succeeding year, new lambs would have to be offered. However, the event had an enduring effect or impact because of God's participation. God's action that first Passover transcended time, as God Himself transcends all time and is able to be present to all history. Thus, because He is God, His Passover action possesses an enduring power that the Israelites could tap into again and again every time they celebrated the feast.

The biblical concept of remembrance becomes even more extraordinary with the New Covenant Passover, which Jesus anticipated and first "pre-presented" at the Last Supper and commanded His Apostles to celebrate thereafter "in remembrance of me" (cf. Lk. 22:15–20).[10] Because there is only one Lamb whose sacrifice culminates in everlasting glory, both the divine blessing and the Passover sacrifice endure in the

---

[10] The God who can culminate His self-offering in everlasting glory in the heavenly sanctuary is also all-powerful enough to offer this same completed, glorified Sacrifice *in advance* of His actual historical death and Resurrection. Similarly, Christ applied the merits of His Sacrifice to His mother in advance of Calvary, preserving her from sin from the moment of her conception.

New Covenant, making Christ's once-for-all self-offering present every time we celebrate the Mass "in memory" of Him. Even more profoundly, because Christ's sacrifice is principally offered in the heavenly sanctuary, we can also say that heaven and earth mysteriously intersect at Mass, enabling us to become present to His everlasting Offering. In other words, Paradise is as close as the next Mass at your local church!

Consider this analogy as a means of further clarification. The sun doesn't actually rise anew each day. Rather, the sun exists *perpetually*, *within time*, and *we* become present anew to this our earth-sustaining life source each day at sunrise, as our world turns on its axis. Similarly, Jesus the Son of God doesn't suffer, die and rise again at each and every Mass, as some Protestant Christians misunderstand. Rather, the completed sacrifice of the Lamb, who was slain, *transcends time itself* and thus is celebrated *forever* in heaven (Rev. 5:11–14). Therefore, every time we "remember" Jesus at Mass, we are able to become present to, and to re-present anew to the Father, from our perspective, the never-ending and eternally life-giving Offering of His Son. While time passes, Christ's sacrifice of Calvary remains the same (cf. Heb. 13:8), the quintessential Gift that keeps on giving (cf. *Catechism*, no. 1085).

In summary, Christ's historical sacrifice on Calvary cannot be isolated from its liturgical completion in heaven. As Frank Sheed concisely observed, "The essence of the Mass is that Christ is making an offering to the Father of Himself, who was slain for us upon Calvary. The Mass is Calvary, *as Christ now offers it to His Father*."[11]

---

[11] Frank Sheed, *Theology and Sanity*, 2nd ed. (Huntington, IN: Our Sunday Visitor, 1978), 231, emphasis in original.

A Foretaste of Heaven

As noted earlier, the Jewish Passover sacrifice was not simply offered but was also eaten. The author of Hebrews makes a profound link between Christ's Offering of Calvary, and how it will be re-presented and consumed thereafter—in a Melchizedekian fashion: "In the days of His flesh, Jesus offered up prayers and supplications, with loud cries and tears, to him who was able to save him from death, and he was heard for his godly fear. Although He was a Son, he learned obedience through what he suffered; and being made perfect he became the source of eternal salvation to all who obey him, being designated by God a high priest after the order of Melchizedek" (Heb. 5:7–10).

In proclaiming that Christ's perfect sacrifice made Him the source of eternal salvation forever and, thereby, a priest forever according to the order of Melchizedek (cf. Heb. 5:9–10), the author of Hebrews affirms that Calvary and the Last Supper are intimately linked in a truly sublime, sacrificial manner. Christ Himself explicitly linked the Last Supper event with His imminent sacrifice of Calvary, offering His Body and Blood under the Melchizedekian signs of bread and wine (Lk. 22:19–20; cf. Gen. 14:18). The author of Hebrews further tells us that Christ's Melchizedekian priesthood was enacted in light of Calvary, indicating that Jesus somehow continues His priestly ministry of Calvary, that is, the work of eternal salvation, in a Melchizedekian manner.

As noted earlier, Saint Paul corroborates that the memorial of the Last Supper is a sacrifice offered in a Melchizedekian manner, that is, under the appearances of bread and wine (cf. 1 Cor. 10:14–22; 11:17–34).[12] Furthermore, as with the Old Covenant, the New Covenant is ratified by the faithful's communion with the Blood of the sacrificial victim, except a more intimate Eucharistic consumption has fulfilled the more ancient covering with blood (cf. Ex. 24:5–8).

Indeed, Jesus promises eternal life to those who reverently eat His Body and drink His Blood (cf. Jn. 6:53–58). As the Lamb of God, who takes away the sin of the world through His once-for-all, yet everlasting sacrifice, He is worthy of our trust.

Thomas J. Nash has a long affiliation with Catholics United for the Faith (CUF). He is the author of Worthy Is the Lamb: The Biblical Roots of the Mass *(Ignatius Press). Tom has worked in both the secular media and the Catholic press, with articles appearing in such publications as* Lay Witness, Catholic World Report, *and* This Rock. *He has also represented CUF to various media, including* Inside the Vatican, U.S. News & World Report, *and* The New York Times. *He has a B.A. in Communications (University of Michigan); an M.A. in Journalism (University of Missouri); and an M.A. in Theology (Franciscan University of Steubenville).*

CHAPTER V

From Jewish Passover to Christian Eucharist
The Todah Sacrifice as Backdrop for the Last Supper

TIM GRAY

Introduction

What is more Jewish than the Passover, or more Christian than the celebration of the Eucharist? These two remarkable religions give birth to liturgies that, in their turn, form and nourish the religious character of their adherents. Those who partake of the tables of Passover and Eucharist not only consume a sacred meal, they digest a distinctive and deep religious identity. Participants walk away not only nourished by the meal but, even more, by the meaning manifest in the meal's ritual signs. The food and drink contain more than calories, they convey the story celebrated and inseparable from the feast. Bread and wine both serve to celebrate and signify a story—indeed the primordial story of each faith, Jewish and Christian.

How did the bread and wine become intertwined with the narrative story that they celebrate? How did the Eucharist arise from the practice of the Passover? More specifically, did Jesus intend to change the Passover into a different feast altogether? What relationship did Jesus' Last Supper have with the Passover? Or, for that matter, what did Eucharist have to do—in the minds of the first Christians—with the Last Supper, not to mention its Jewish antecedent, the Passover?

Scholars have often pondered as to how the practice of Christian Eucharist could have arisen from the Lord's Supper that occurred in the context of the Jewish Passover. Since Passover arrived once a year, how is it that the Christians got the notion that they could celebrate Jesus' sacrificial meal weekly, if not daily?

The fact that the Eucharist was immediately unmoored from the Passover also raises questions about continuity. If Jesus' Last Supper was a Passover meal, how can the Christian Eucharist be in continuity with it without reference to the Passover?

There is, indeed, a vital connection between the Passover, Last Supper, and Eucharist. An ancient Jewish sacrifice, known as *todah*, is the chain that links these feasts in such a way that, after a better understanding of todah, we shall see how the Christian Eucharist is anchored in the Jewish Passover. The todah reveals how the Last Supper functions as a bridge between Jewish Passover and Christian Eucharist. To discover these connections, we must begin with a brief examination of the little-known sacrifice known as the todah.

The Todah Sacrifice

Although most Christians have heard of the ancient Jewish sacrifices—burnt offerings, holocaust offerings, or even the cereal and peace offerings—those who have heard of the todah sacrifice are as rare as lotto winners. Current ignorance concerning the todah, however, should not imply that it was unimportant to the Jews. Far from it. The todah was one of the most important and popular sacrifices of the Jews.

Indeed, an old Rabbinic dictum makes this point well: "In the coming Messianic age all sacrifices will cease, but the thank offering [todah] will never cease."[1] Certainly the sole sacrifice to survive the advent of the Messiah must have held some weight for the Jews.

Todah as Jewish Name: Judah

What does the word "todah" mean? To begin with, the word "todah" is Hebrew for "thanksgiving," although it also connotes a confession of praise as well as gratitude. For example, Leah gives thanks to God when she bears her fourth son, and so she names him *yehudah*—or Judah—which is the verbal form of todah—to give thanks. So the term *Judah* means to give thanks to God, which is interesting given that many of the psalms of thanksgiving are ascribed to David, of the tribe of Judah.

---

[1] Taken from the Pesiqta, quoted in Hartmut Gese, *Essays on Biblical Theology* (Minneapolis: Augsburg, 1981).

Example: Hezekiah

A todah sacrifice would be offered by someone
whose life had been delivered from great peril,
whether disease or the sword. The person redeemed
would show his gratitude to God by gathering his
closest friends and family for a todah sacrificial
meal. A lamb would be sacrificed in the Temple,
and the bread for the meal would be consecrated
the moment the lamb was sacrificed.[2] The bread
and meat, along with wine, would constitute the
elements of the sacred todah meal, which would be
accompanied by prayers and songs of thanksgiving,
such as Psalm 116. The meal would be a joy-filled
feast, celebrating God's goodness and love with song,
story, and music.

A good example of a todah celebration is found
in the story of Hezekiah, who fell deathly ill amidst
the siege upon Jerusalem by Sennacherib, king of
Assyria (Is. 37–38). Hezekiah, at the point of death,
cries out to the Lord in prayer and supplication for
healing and deliverance. Isaiah declares to Hezekiah
God's answer: both he and the city of Jerusalem will
be delivered (Is. 38:6). After Hezekiah recovers from
his illness he composes a todah song to honor and
give thanks to God for his and the city's miraculous
deliverance (Is. 38:9–20).

The song begins with a lament that recounts
Hezekiah's suffering (38:10–15). Then he relates
how he cried out to the Lord (38:16–18), which is
followed by a promise and a call to give thanks for
the rest of his life (38:19–20). Note how the giving

---

[2] For example, the Mishnah Menahot 2:3; 7:2–4, in Jacob Neusner,
trans., *The Mishnah: A New Translation* (New Haven, CT: Yale
University Press, 1988), 746–47.

of thanks is not seen as a one-time event, but rather the todah celebration marks a new way of life—a life now dedicated to giving praise and thanks forever:

> The living, the living, he *thanks* thee, as I do this day; the father makes known to the children thy faithfulness.
>
> The LORD will save me, and we will sing to stringed instruments all the days of our life, at the house of the LORD. (38:19–20, emphasis added)

Notice how Hezekiah promises to sing the praises of God in thanksgiving for "all the days of our life." This illustrates how the todah celebration was the beginning of a life dedicated to grateful praise to God, a life that would witness to God's saving deeds, making "known to the children your faithfulness." In this story the deliverance of the ill king is a sign also of God's deliverance of an ill people (Is. 1:4–9), whose sin is pardoned by the deliverance of their city—a deliverance that should bring about a new life dedicated to gratitude and service to God.

The example of Hezekiah illustrates the typical pattern of the todah. For instance, someone finds himself in a life-threatening situation, encountering serious sufferings. Then he calls out to the Lord with a lament, recounting his bitter experience to God. This lament is accompanied with hope and faith, as the sufferer calls out to God for deliverance. The Lord answers with deliverance, and the lament turns into praise and thanksgiving. The one who has been redeemed gathers friends and family (notice the "we" of Hezekiah's psalm, describing the corporate aspect of those who go to the Temple to sing God's praises) to give thanks to God with a public demonstration of praise, which is marked with testimony of God's faithfulness and loving kindness. This is the pattern of todah, the pattern of Israel's praise.[3]

David's Todah Liturgy

After David had defeated the last Canaanite stronghold, he decided to bring the Ark of the Covenant up to Jerusalem. This event was the occasion of a great national todah festival. The narrative account mentions that the sacrifices were "peace offerings," which is the general category of which the todah is the most important and common peace offering (cf. 2 Sam. 6:18 and 1 Chron. 16). The peace offerings are offered in thanksgiving, which fits the description of peace offerings as todah in Leviticus 7:11–18.

It is clear that David offered up the peace offerings as a todah celebration because all the elements of the todah are found in the event. David offers bread and wine along with the meat of the sacrifices: "And he dealt to every one of Israel, both man and woman, to every one a loaf of bread, and a good piece of flesh, and a flagon *of wine*" (1 Chron. 16:3, KJV translation, emphasis added). Most importantly, we are told that David had the Levites lead the people in todah hymns, that is, in psalms of thanksgiving (1 Chron. 16:8–36).

Why did Israel gather as a nation to celebrate thanksgiving while David brought the Ark into Jerusalem? They rejoice because David had accomplished something that Joshua had started, and no one prior to David had been able to finish—the conquest

---

[3] Note that praise and thanks are often interchangeable terms in the todah, for example, in Hezekiah's psalm they are used in synonymous parallelism (Is. 38:18).

of the Promised Land and complete defeat of the Canaanites. David now had "rest" from his enemies, and so the injunction of Deuteronomy 12 could come into play—they could now establish a place for God's name to dwell—that is the Temple. So the thanksgiving celebration marked the end of the era of conquest and struggle begun by Joshua, while at the same time, it ushered in the era of kingdom building.

At this pivotal point in Israel's story, David not only changes the location of the ark, but he also transforms Israel's liturgy. David introduces a kind of "*novus ordo*," a new order to the liturgy. At the todah celebration that brought the Ark into Jerusalem, David gave the Levites a new mandate—their primary job was to "invoke, to thank, and to praise the LORD" (1 Chron. 16:4). Notice the key terms that accompany the thanksgiving: "invoke" and "praise." The Hebrew word for "invoke" is *zakar*, which literally means to remember; the noun form signifies "memorial" (*zikkaron*). One of the most important purposes of a todah meal was to recall the saving deeds of the Lord. Indeed, this is one of the functions of the todah psalms, which serve to recount the mighty deeds of God (e.g. Ps. 22 28). We are also informed, "Then on that day David first appointed that thanksgiving (todah) be sung to the Lord by Asaph and his brethren" (1 Chron. 16:7). The Levites were to give thanks and praise to God "continually" (*tamid* in the Hebrew) (16:37, 40). This perpetual adoration was to characterize the Temple liturgy as a todah liturgy—a liturgy of thanksgiving.[4]

---

[4] The prayers for the morning and evening sacrifice were characterized by the todah thanksgiving (1 Chron. 16:40–41). See also Allan Bouley's discussion of how the prayers at the morning and evening sacrifices

Todah Shape of the Psalter

The Psalter made up the heart of the hymns and prayers of the Temple liturgy. In light of the account in Chronicles where David appointed the Levites to give perpetual thanks, we can see why it has been observed that "the thank offering constituted the cultic basis for the main bulk of the Psalms."[5] The todah Psalms have a twofold structure. First, although they may begin with thanks and praise, the first half of the song is largely a lament, where the psalmist recounts how his life was in peril. Then the psalmist recounts how God graciously heard his plea and brought about deliverance from death. Thus the second part of the song, or at the least its conclusion, is usually taken up with giving thanks and praise to God.[6] So the movement of the todah Psalms is from plight to praise—a movement that reflects Israel's movement from enslavement to exodus—while also looking forward to the paschal mystery of our Lord.

Todah and Jesus

The importance of the todah as a backdrop for Jesus and the Last Supper comes into sharp focus when one realizes that in Jesus' day the Greek word that would best translate the Hebrew *todah* was *eucharistia*, the Greek word from which we get the word "Eucharist." *Eucharistia*, like todah, means thanksgiving. From the earliest Christian sources, it

---

included thanksgiving formulas in *From Freedom to Formula: The Evolution of the Eucharistic Prayer from Oral Improvisation to Written Texts* (Washington, DC: Catholic University of America Press, 1981), 7–13.

[5] Gese, 131.

[6] Some examples from the multitude of todah psalms are Psalms 16, 18, 21, 32, 65, 100, 107, 116, 124, 136.

becomes evident that Christians identified the celebration of the Lord's meal, or what we call the Mass, as the Eucharist. In one of the earliest accounts of the Christian celebration of the Eucharist, around AD 155, Justin Martyr constantly repeats the Greek term *eucharistia*, thanksgiving:

> [H]e taking them [bread and wine], gives praise and glory to the Father of the universe, through the name of the Son and of the Holy Ghost, and offers thanks [*eucharistian*] at considerable length for our being counted worthy to receive these things at His hands. And when he has concluded the prayers and thanksgivings, all the people present express their assent by saying Amen. . . . And when the president has given thanks and the people expressed their assent, those who are called by us deacons give to each of those present to partake of the bread and wine mixed with water over which the thanksgiving was pronounced, and to those who are absent they carry away a portion.[7]

The idea that the thanksgiving was the defining characteristic of the consecration of the bread and wine arose because, at the Last Supper, Jesus took the bread and wine and gave "thanks" (*eucharistia*) over them (Lk. 22:19).

Indeed, the *Catechism* describes the Mass as a sacrifice of thanksgiving to the Father: "The Eucharist is a sacrifice of thanksgiving to the Father, a blessing by which the Church expresses her gratitude to God for all his benefits, for all that he has accomplished through creation, redemption, and sanctification. Eucharist means first of all 'thanks-

---

[7] Saint Justin Martyr, *Apologia I*, chap. LXV, in *Ante-Nicene Fathers*, vol.1, eds. Alexander Roberts and James Donaldson (Peabody, MA: Hendrickson, 1994), 185.

giving'" (*Catechism*, no. 1360). Thus, it is clear that "thanksgiving" is at the heart of the Eucharistic feast, but does this relate to the ancient Hebrew sacrifice of thanksgiving?

The German biblical scholar Hartmut Gese claimed that the todah stands behind what Jesus did at the Last Supper. He goes so far as to argue that Jesus' giving thanks over the bread and wine came in the context of a todah sacrifice rather than a Passover meal. No other Scripture scholars, however, have followed Gese's suggestions about the todah backdrop of Jesus' meal, because the evidence for the Passover in the Gospel narratives is overwhelming.

Here is where I would like to make an adjustment to Gese's theory. I think he is right to see the todah backdrop, but wrong to deny the larger Passover context. The solution to the seeming dilemma is actually quite easy. The Last Supper, celebrated in the upper room, is both a Passover and todah meal. The Passover has all the same elements found in the todah: bread, wine, sacrifice of a lamb, along with hymns and prayers. Indeed, the Hallel Psalms, 113–118, that were sung during the Passover meal were all todah Psalms! The Exodus narrative itself has the basic contours of a todah hymn, with Israel in distress and lament calling out to the Lord (cf. Ex. 2:23–25), while the Lord in turn hears their cry and delivers them (cf. Ex. 6:5–7). The Passover has both the form and content of the todah because it is a concrete example of a todah sacrifice.

Philo, a first-century Jew, describes the purpose of the Passover festival as thanksgiving: "And this festival is instituted in remembrance of, and as giving thanks for, their great migration which they made from

Egypt."[8] Philo focuses here on two key reasons for the Passover, remembrance and thanksgiving. The notion of remembrance was always an essential element of the Passover from the beginning (cf. Ex. 12:14; 13:3). Here again we must note how the Passover fits into the todah genre, for remembrance was one of the primary purposes of the todah. In discussing the purpose of the Passover as thanksgiving, it is worth noting that Philo, who writes in Greek, employs the term *eucharistia*. The Passover then is the meal of thanksgiving where the Israelites confess how God redeemed them from Egyptian bondage. The Passover is Israel's corporate todah meal.

When Jesus takes the bread, breaks it, and declares thanksgiving (*eucharistia*), he is performing the key function of both the todah and Passover—giving thanks for deliverance. Here, however, Jesus is not simply looking back at Israel's history of salvation, but forward to His death and Resurrection. In other words, Jesus is giving thanks to the Father for His love and for the new life to be granted in the Resurrection. Note that Jesus' words over the bread, His thanksgiving, are what the Christian tradition has focused upon. Thus they could call every re-enactment of the Last Supper, "Eucharist."

In the Eucharist, Christians, as the Jews did with Passover, give thanks for God's deliverance and bring to remembrance how Jesus brought about the New Exodus with His death and Resurrection. For Jesus had told them, "Do this in remembrance of me" (Lk. 22:19). This act of remembrance is what the todah is all about—remembering in gratitude God's

---

[8]   Philo, *The Special Laws*, bk. II, 145, in *The Works of Philo*, trans. C. D. Young (Peabody, MA: Hendrickson, 1993), 582.

saving deeds. This leads us to one of the key fruits of a todah and of Eucharistic spirituality. A deep sense of thankfulness leads to worship. Worship flows from gratitude. If gratitude is cut off, the will to worship will wither.

But it is the lesson of the todah that teaches us to trust God with a grateful heart. By recalling and "remembering" Jesus' gift of Himself upon the Cross and in the Eucharist, our love for God is rekindled. Such "remembrance," which is the purpose of todah, leads to deeper trust. As the psalmist says, "Some trust in chariots, and some in horses: but we will remember the name of the LORD our God" (Ps. 20:7).[9] By participating in Jesus' Eucharistic thanksgiving, we remember who God is, and so we learn to trust in the love that moves the sun and the stars. That is what a Eucharistic spirituality is all about.

Tim Gray is the director of the Denver Catholic Biblical School and a professor of Scripture at St. John Vianney Seminary. He has a Th.M. in Scripture from Duke University and is close to completing his Ph.D. studies at Catholic University of America. Tim frequently appears on EWTN, and is the author of Mission of the Messiah, *(Emmaus Road) a Bible study of the Gospel of Luke,* Sacraments in Scripture, *(Emmaus Road) and coauthor of* Boys to Men: The Transforming Power of Virtue *(Emmaus Road).*

CHAPTER VI

Time *for* Liturgy
"Appointed Times" in Judaism and Christianity

SEAN INNERST

The Year of Grace

There is nothing quite so distinctive about Catholic life as our yearly round of feasts and fasts that we call the Liturgical Year. Having been raised in a Protestant denomination that observed no real holy days apart from the weekly Sunday observance, which we called "First Day," it has been a joy to come to appreciate the punctuation of time by the recollection of the great works of God in history that makes the Christian calendar truly a "year of grace." Although when I was growing up we often made concessions to the common cultural practices surrounding Christmas and Easter, the position of Quakerism from its foundations was that every day is a day of grace and so no day should be held above another. A statement from a group of primitive Quakers made a decade or so ago framed the issue this way:

As we hold that one day is no more holy than
another, as all days are the gift of the most High,
do we continue to maintain a firm Christian witness that our members do not join in any public
fasts, feasts, so-called holy-days and religious festivals (such as times called "Christmas" and "Easter"
by some); for though exterior observances of a
similar kind were once authorized under the law,
as shadows of things to come, yet they who come
to Christ will we believe assuredly find that in him
all shadows end.[1]

That last reference to "shadows" is an allusion to
Saint Paul's Letter to the Colossians where, in reference to the Jewish rituals celebrated before Christ's
coming, he says, "These are only a shadow of what
is to come; but the substance belongs to Christ"
(Col. 2:17). As the quote above from just one group
of Quaker traditionalists would suggest, to many
Christians that phrase from Saint Paul asserts that
all of the previous practice of Judaism in celebrating
particular days of the year with rituals we could call
liturgies[2] has been abolished with Christ's coming.

---

[1] Yearly Meeting of Friends in Christ, *Queries and Advice Also Containing a Concise Account of Our Beliefs and Tenets and a Statement of Faith* (1993), as quoted in Bill Samuel, "Friends (Quakers) and Christmas"; http://www.quakerinfo.com/quakxmas.shtml.

[2] "Liturgy (*leitourgia*) is a Greek composite word meaning originally a public duty, a service to the state undertaken by a citizen. Its elements are *leitos* (from *leos* = *laos*, people) meaning *public*, and *ergo* (obsolete in the present stem, used in future *erxo*, etc.), *to do*. From this we have *leitourgos*, "a man who performs a public duty", "a public servant". . . . The meaning of the word liturgy is then extended to cover any general service of a public kind. In the Septuagint it (and the verb *leitourgeo*) is used for the public service of the temple (e.g., Ex., xxxviii, 27; xxxix, 12, etc.). Thence it comes to have a religious sense as the function of the priests, the ritual service of the temple (e. g., Joel, i, 9; ii, 17, etc.). In the New Testament this religious meaning has become definitely established. In Luke, i, 23, Zachary goes home when "the days of his *liturgy*" (*ai hemerai tes leitourgias autou*) are over. In Heb., viii, 6, the high priest

I've come to see in my study of the Scriptures, however, that while the feasts, fasts, and liturgies of Judaism, what Saint Paul calls the "shadow" have been replaced by the "substance" of worship in Christ, that doesn't mean that all liturgy nor the liturgical cycle have been altogether abolished in the Christian age. To use Paul's metaphor, a shadow resembles the object of which it is but a mere outline. But a shadow does have the same contours, the same shape or form as that of which it is a representation. If the shadow consists of ritual actions performed at regular intervals in a yearly cycle, then wouldn't the "substance" that casts the shadow have the same form?[3]

This chapter is intended to show the relationship between the shadow, Jewish ritual life, and the substance, Christian worship since Christ's coming as man. I've found that not only is there a continuity between the worship of the Jews and that of the Catholic Church, but that there is even a suggestion in the creation narrative that the yearly round of seasons was intended by God from the beginning to be marked by a cycle of ritual feasts—in short, that time itself is for liturgy.

---

of the New Law "has obtained a better *liturgy*", that is a better kind of public religious service than that of the Temple.

"So in Christian use liturgy meant the public official service of the Church, that corresponded to the official service of the Temple in the Old Law." From the article "Liturgy" in The Catholic Encyclopedia, vol. 9 (New York: Encyclopedia Press, 1913); http://www.newadvent.org/cathen/09306a.htm.

[3] For a full treatment on the application of this Pauline metaphor in the work of the Fathers, see Jean Cardinal Daniélou's *From Shadows to Reality: Studies in the Biblical Typology of the Fathers* (Westminster, MD: Newman Press, 1960).

The "Sevening" of Time

The more I read the Scriptures, the more I am
convinced that one of the most fundamental texts is
the one which Jesus speaks at the very heart of the
Sermon on the Mount: "Think not that I have come
to abolish the law and the prophets; I have come
not to abolish them but to fulfill them" (Mt. 5:17).
This verse is a kind of theme verse for Matthew,
whose Gospel is singularly concerned with the way
in which Jesus is simultaneously in perfect continuity with the Jewish past, and an absolute surprise to
Jewish expectations. It is also a veritable theme verse
for the whole of the ancient Church's interpretation
of the Scriptures.

Matthew's Gospel was cited almost exclusively
by the Fathers of the Church for the first couple of
Christian centuries. And just as Matthew moves back
and forth between the Old Testament and Jesus' fulfillment of it, so also the scriptural interpretation of
the first centuries, and in fact, for most of the history
of the Church, will move to the same rhythm, finding
the New hidden in the Old, and the Old made manifest in the New.

In what may well be a kind of signature verse
for Matthew, scribe of the Gospel that he was, he
quotes Jesus as saying, "Therefore every scribe who
has been trained for the kingdom of heaven is like a
householder who brings out of his treasure what is
new and what is old" (Mt. 13:52). Whether as just
a dictum that Matthew and those who came after
him seemed intent on following or as a prophetic
utterance in the fuller sense, Christ's words find fulfillment in Matthew's own mode of interpretation of
the events of the revelation. He structures much of

his Gospel around this principle of fulfillment of the Old Testament in the New. And the other Gospel writers too seem intent on making the same kinds of connections.

One of the things that Christ came to fulfill was the feasts of the liturgical year of ancient Judaism. These are delineated in the twenty-third chapter of Leviticus. There the Lord tells Moses, "Say to the people of Israel, The appointed feasts of the LORD which you shall proclaim as holy convocations, my appointed feasts, are these" (Lev. 23:2). The first bedrock observance is, of course, the Sabbath of solemn rest that sanctifies each week. The Sabbath observance had been enjoined in the Ten Commandments (Ex. 20:11); it is also assumed in the event of the provision of manna in Exodus 16. That miraculous bread, which normally went foul if kept until the next day, was both unavailable for gathering on the Sabbath and was preserved for the Sabbath from the previous day. And, of course, the Pentateuch sees the roots of the Sabbath observance in the account of creation itself, as seen in Genesis 2:3: "So God blessed the seventh day and hallowed it, because on it God rested from all his work which he had done in creation" (Ex. 31:12–17).

This "sevening" or sabbath blessing is played out again and again in the process of sanctifying time in the Old Testament. In Leviticus 25, God commands that every seventh year, in effect a sabbath of years, be observed with a solemn rest from plowing and pruning, for man and beast. God even calls for a jubilee year after "seven weeks of years" (7 x 7 = 49), that is, in the fiftieth year, beginning on the first day of the feast of Atonement, during which the Jews are to rest from labor for a whole year and to offer return of land and freedom to those who had lost either because of debt or sale since the last major jubilee.

This "sevening" of time can be seen, too, in the yearly feasts of Israel, of which there were seven commanded in Leviticus 23. Three of these, Passover (*Pesach*), Unleavened Bread (*Matzot*), and First Fruits, were celebrated in the first month of the Jewish calendar, Nisan, which falls in the spring. They combined the commemoration of the first Passover with a memorial of the first harvest in the Promised Land. One other feast, that of Weeks (*Shavuot*), fell one day beyond seven weeks after First Fruits (again, 7 x 7 days + 1, or 50 days) and so was, and still is, called Pentecost, from the Greek word for fifty days. It celebrates both the full harvest and the giving of the law at Mount Sinai.

The three other feasts, Trumpets (*Rosh Hashanah*), Atonement (*Yom Kippur*), and Tabernacles or Booths (*Succoth*), were celebrated during Tishri, the seventh month of the year. These last three constitute the High Holy Days of Judaism. Trumpets signal not only the start of the civil year, as opposed to the liturgical year, but also the "ten days of awe," that period of repentance leading up to the feast of Atonement. Jewish tradition has it that those who are neither in the book of the righteous nor the book of the unrighteous have ten days to reform before the books and their fate are sealed on the feast of Atonement. On that day, the High Priest offered sacrifices of atonement for sin, for himself and his family, and then for the whole people, entering the holy of holies for the only time during the year to offer incense and to sprinkle the blood of the animal sacrifices on the Mercy Seat. Afterwards, he would bless the people, pronouncing the divine name, *YHWH* (typically pronounced "Yahweh") over them, a name which was reserved for this feast alone, and which was otherwise never spoken.

Tabernacles, which begins five days after Atonement, is also a seven-day memorial feast commemorating the Exodus, with a solemn rest observed on the eighth day. Great menorahs were lit in the Court of the Women, illuminating the Temple Mount, and on the eighth day, the High Priest would pour water from Siloam on the altar as a prayer for the fall rains. This feast also marked the ingathering from the threshing floor and the wine press (cf. Deut. 16:13) and so came to take on eschatological significance as a figure for the gathering of all of God's people in the messianic age, and also for the judgment at the end of time (cf. Rev. 14:14–20).

These seven feasts divide the year into two great blocks of feasts in the first and seventh months, in the spring and fall, with Pentecost standing on its own in late May or June. Three of the seven feasts, Passover, Pentecost, and Tabernacles, were called pilgrim feasts because able-bodied men were expected to come to Jerusalem for their observance (Ex. 23:14–17). In this way, the year was punctuated by religious celebrations that served as a kind of life breath of Judaism as she inhaled her pilgrims into the Jerusalem Temple and exhaled them out again into the towns and villages of Israel, and even into the diaspora beyond.

As was mentioned above, these feasts were commanded by God. By them, God was claiming a place in the lives of His people and was hallowing time. These feasts served to keep the founding events of

Mosaic Judaism, the events of the Exodus, deeply etched in the memory of the Jews. But they were not merely memorial. They also pointed forward to some sort of fulfillment in a future messianic age.

A Feast of Fulfillments

How then, we might ask, did Jesus fulfill these seven feasts? On the surface level, Jesus apparently participated in the yearly round of Jewish feasts. Even as a child, as Luke tells us, He went "to Jerusalem every year at the feast of the Passover" with His parents (2:41). In his Gospel, John even marks the passing of the public ministry of Jesus by the passage of the feasts, especially Passover, which Jesus as an adult still observed as a pilgrim feast. At a deeper level, however, we see that Jesus also used the occasion of the various feasts to teach particular lessons and to accomplish certain parts of His messianic mission, investing the Jewish feasts with an enduring Christian significance. The most striking instance of this occurs at the time of Jesus' Passion, death, and Resurrection. Jesus' condemnation and death occurs at the time of the Passover. We observe Holy Thursday as a Christian memorial of the Passover Seder that Jesus celebrated the evening before He died. With the words, "Do this in remembrance of me," Jesus made the Passover a continual ritual or liturgical feast.

The New Testament calls this memorial feast "breaking bread" and the day of its weekly celebration the "Lord's Day" (cf. Acts 20:7–11; Rev. 1:10). This observance, as the *Catechism of the Catholic Church* points out, "replaces that of the sabbath" (no. 2175) as can also be seen from the earliest post-biblical Christian texts. The Catechism cites

Saint Ignatius of Antioch's *Letter to the Magnesians*, written in about AD 110, and Saint Justin Martyr's *First Apology*, written about fifty years later, explaining the reason for the transference of the Sabbath to Sunday, from the seventh day of the week to the first day. This transference indicates that the fulfilling work of Christ pushes us beyond the last day of creation to a new day of re-creation in Christ (cf. *Catechism*, nos. 2174–75).

The Sunday observance of what the Bible calls "the Lord's Day" expressed for the early Christians the whole movement from Judaism to the new Way, from creation to new creation, from law to grace, and from time to eternity—all accomplished by the saving work of Christ. This weekly celebration, which the *Catechism* calls "the foremost obligation in the universal Church" (no. 2177, quoting Code of Canon Law, can.1246 § 1), is the new anchor of the Christian liturgical year, as was the earlier Sabbath celebration for the Jews. While it is true that the Church daily celebrates the new memorial celebration that we call the Mass, the Sunday celebration is the primary weekly reliving of the Paschal Mystery of Christ and is in a real way a mini-Easter.[4]

---

[4] A possible warrant for the daily celebration of the Breaking of Bread, the Lord's Supper or Mass, can be found in Acts 2:42 and 46, which report that after Pentecost the first Christians "devoted themselves to the apostle's teaching and fellowship, to the breaking of bread and prayers," and that "day by day, attending the temple together and breaking bread in their homes, they partook of food with glad and generous hearts." Some commentators see this as a witness that, even in the earliest Church, the breaking of bread as a ritual memorial of Christ's Passion, death, and Resurrection was conducted daily.

On the issue of the transference of the Jewish Sabbath to Sunday, see also the argument made in Hebrews 3 and 4, which seems to be asserting to Jewish Christians tempted to return to Jewish patterns of worship that, while the exodus generation of Israel had been promised a "rest,"

Each Mass re-presents the Last Supper, at which
Jesus offered His Body and Blood in anticipation of
His perfect sacrifice on the Cross the next day. The
precious Body and Blood which He offered His apostles at that Supper, and which we receive at Holy
Communion, is the resurrected and glorified body
that Jesus possesses forever in heaven. And so each
and every Mass encompasses all the events from the
Last Supper to Good Friday to Easter Sunday. Jesus'
institution of the Mass fulfills—and in a rather stunning way—all of the Jewish feasts that occurred on
those same days in the month of Nisan in the year of
His death and rising.

The Triduum's Triple Fulfillment

Furthermore, the feasts of Holy Week—Holy
Thursday, Good Friday, Holy Saturday, and Easter—
are fulfillments of the three spring Jewish feasts with
which they originally coincided. We refer to the three
great liturgies of Holy Week—the Mass of the Lord's
Supper on Holy Thursday evening, Good Friday services, and the Easter Vigil—as the Holy Triduum. In
the year of Christ's death, the Jewish Passover on 14
Nisan would have begun at sundown on Thursday,
the same evening as the celebration of the Last Supper
and been completed at sundown on Good Friday, the
day of His death.

----

of which the (Saturday) Sabbath was a sign, because of disobedience
that rest had never been obtained. Then, in an apparent reference to the
new Christian regime of the Sunday observance, the author of Hebrews
says, "there remains a sabbath rest for the people of God; for whoever
enters God's rest also ceases from his labours as God did from his. Let
us therefore strive to enter that rest, that no one fall by the same sort of
disobedience" (4:9–11).

What we call Holy Saturday, the day that Christ lay in the tomb, a day without its own liturgy, coincides with the first day of the feast of Unleavened Bread on 15 Nisan, which is closely associated with Passover. Leaven, a sign of sin, is cleansed from all Jewish homes on the eve of Passover. And the following seven days of Unleavened Bread, called in Deuteronomy 16:3 "the bread of affliction," are observed, beginning the day after Passover, as a memorial of the flight from Egypt and as a reminder to each Jew "of what the Lord did for me when I came out of Egypt" (Ex. 13:8).

The feast of First Fruits, which coincided that year with the day of Christ's Resurrection and commemorated the first sheaf of the barley harvest, began after sundown of 15 Nisan (according to Jewish reckoning the beginning of 16 Nisan). This feast, involving a ceremonial cutting and offering of the first fruit of this harvest, asks God's blessing in anticipation of the full harvest in the spring at the Feast of Weeks or Pentecost.

To sum up, Jesus died on the afternoon of Passover, a day on which a lamb was slain and eaten to commemorate the sparing of the firstborn of Israel during the tenth plague in Egypt. Just as the blood of the lamb was placed on the doorposts of the households of Israel to ensure their salvation as the angel of death struck the firstborn of Egypt, so now in Christ, the blood of the slain Lamb of God saves us from the death of sin.[5] On the day we call Holy Saturday, while

_____

[5] According to the requirements for the Passover feast outlined in Exodus 12, the Passover lamb was to be set apart from the flock on the tenth day of the month and kept in the household until its sacrifice on the fourteenth day. That tenth day would have coincided with the triumphal entry of Jesus into the city of Jerusalem on Palm Sunday. So,

the Jews celebrated the rejection of sin on the feast of Unleavened Bread, the body of Jesus, who had offered Himself to His apostles as the bread of life at the Last Supper and had definitively defeated sin by His death on the Cross, lay in the tomb. On Easter Sunday morning, Jesus revealed Himself as what Saint Paul would later call "the first fruits of those who have fallen asleep" (1 Cor. 15:20). And this He did on the very day that the Jews called First Fruits! So, Jesus instituted the Eucharist and died on Passover, lay buried during the feast of Unleavened Bread, and rose on First Fruits.

As we know from the account in Acts 2, on the first Christian Pentecost—the day during which the Jews were celebrating the harvest and the giving of the Law on Mount Sinai fifty days after the Exodus—the promise of the first fruits, seen in Christ's Resurrection, finds its fulfillment in the sending of the Holy Spirit and a harvest of three thousand souls from every nation of the Jewish diaspora. It is worth noting that, at the giving of the Law at Mount Sinai, three thousand died as a consequence of their failure of faith and the subsequent idolatrous worship of the golden calf (Ex. 32:28), whereas on this fulfillment of the Jewish Pentecost, three thousand die to sin in the waters of Baptism and come to new life in the Risen Christ (cf. Act 2:38–42).

Filling Out the Fulfillments

It's not uncommon for Christian commentators to suggest that, having fulfilled these four Jewish spring

---

just as Israel was choosing its lambs for slaughter, Jesus was likewise being chosen by the crowds who acclaimed Him. Four days later, on the Passover day celebrating God's sparing of the firstborn, His firstborn Son will spare Himself nothing in saving us.

feasts, Jesus will fulfill the other three—Trumpets, Atonement, and Tabernacles—when He comes again in glory.[6] These three feasts neatly express the events foretold for the end of time: a trumpet blast, judgment, and the gathering of the just into heaven. While it may well be true that their *final* fulfillment will wait for Christ's Second Coming, it is important to recognize that Jesus often used the occasion of these and other feasts to impart important elements of His message, suggesting a kind of provisional fulfillment. One example is the Feast of the Dedication of the Temple, or what is commonly called Chanukah today. This is a later feast than the seven principal feasts we have been considering, instituted in 164 BC to celebrate the purification and rededication of the Temple by Judas Maccabeus after its profanation by Antiochus Epiphanes (cf. 2 Mac. 10). It was at the time of this eight-day feast, which includes the reading of passages from the prophet Ezekiel speaking of God coming as shepherd and judge under a new Davidic king (cf. Ezek. 34:15–25), that Jesus chose to say of Himself, "I am the good shepherd" (Jn. 10:11, see also 10:22). It is during this same feast, which is also called the festival of lights, that Jesus announces, "I am the light of the world" (Jn 9:5).

---

[6] Many Evangelical Protestants believe that Christ fulfilled the first four feasts of Judaism, the Passover, Unleavened Bread, and First Fruits in His death, burial, and Resurrection and then Pentecost in the foundation of the Church, but they claim that the last three will only be fulfilled at the time of the rapture, millennial reign, and final judgment. A Catholic interpretation would, of course, deny entirely the non-biblical and non-traditional belief in the rapture as a pre-, mid- or post-tribulation event other than that indicated by Scripture as belonging to the coincident events of the Second Coming and the final, general judgment. Likewise, the modern dispensationalist innovation, which expects an earthly millennial reign by Christ in His glorified flesh, is entirely foreign to ancient Christianity as well. (See Mt. 24, Mk. 13 and Lk. 21.)

John's Gospel also tells us that Jesus used the
occasion of the last or eighth day of the feast of
Tabernacles, when the High Priest would have been
bathing the altar of the Jerusalem Temple with water,
to announce, "If anyone thirst, let him come to me
and drink. He who believes in me, as the scripture has
said, 'Out of his heart shall flow rivers of living water'"
(Jn. 7:37–38; cf. Ezek. 47:1). It was apparently on the
first day of that same feast, when the great menorah
lights would have been lit in the Temple, that Jesus
led Peter, James, and John to the heights of Mount
Tabor to see Him aglow with a celestial light at the
Transfiguration. Peter offers to build three booths for
Jesus, Moses, and Elijah because it is on that first day
of Tabernacles that the Jews were to take "branches
of palm trees and boughs of leafy trees, and willows
of the brook" and make dwellings like those that the
chosen people had lived in during the Exodus (Lev.
23:40; Mt. 17:1–4). Luke in his account of the same
event seems to strengthen the connection between
Transfiguration and Tabernacles by noting that Moses
and Elijah spoke to Jesus about His impending
"departure," "*exodon*" in the Greek.

Matthew notes in his account that six days before
the Transfiguration (cf. Mt. 17:1), which would have
been the feast of the Atonement, something quite
remarkable took place between Jesus and Peter. Recall
that the feast of the Atonement was the one occasion
when the High Priest was permitted to pronounce the
hallowed name of God, YHWH, which was God's
special revelation of His own identity to Moses on
Mount Sinai. The Revised Standard Version of the
Bible renders the mysterious exchange between God
and Moses and the translation of YHWH in this way:

"Then Moses said to God, 'If I come to the people of Israel and say to them, "The God of your fathers has sent me to you," and they ask me, "What is his name?" what shall I say to them?' God said to Moses, 'I AM WHO I AM.' And he said, 'Say this to the people of Israel, "I am has sent me to you"'" (Ex. 3:13–14).

If "YHWH" or "I AM" is to be the divine name, it is significant that in Matthew 16:15, when Jesus asks the apostles, "[W]ho do you say that *I am*?" (emphasis added), and Simon Peter responds, "You are the Christ, the son of the living God," that Jesus should call it a direct revelation from God the Father. He says to Peter, "Blessed are you, Simon Bar-Jona! For flesh and blood has not revealed this to you, but my Father who is in heaven. And I tell you, you are Peter, and on this rock I will build my church" (Mt. 16:17–18).

This remarkable passage seems to cast Peter, by his disclosure of Jesus' previously hidden identity, in the role of the High Priest, who alone speaks the revealed name on the Day of Atonement. Jesus even calls Peter by his given name "Simon Bar-Jona," which was also the name of a famous High Priest of the Maccabean era whose praises we see sung in a passage in Sirach 50:1–20.[7]

It is worth spending this much time recalling this one fulfillment of a Jewish feast because it shows the

[7] It is interesting that this passage in Sirach is set on the Atonement and makes reference to the High Priestly blessing which involves the pronouncing of the divine Name in the traditional Atonement blessing: "Then Simon came down, and lifted up his hands over the whole congregation of Israel, to pronounce the blessing of the Lord with his lips, and to glory in his name" (Sir. 50:20). For the dating and evaluation of this event, which is so crucial for its proper interpretation, I am drawing on the work of Jean Galot. See his article in *Sacerdos* 2, no. 4 (July–September 1995): 8–11.

coinciding of the feast's fulfillment with the establishment of the authority of Peter and the foundation
of the Church. This new Church, of which Peter is to
be the rock foundation, will be the heir of the feasts of
the Jewish liturgical year, transformed and perfected
in Christ, and the agent in the establishment of the
new liturgy that will fulfill the old.

While we cannot say that Christ, during His earthly ministry, specifically instituted the Catholic calendar
of liturgical celebrations, we can say that by observing
the calendar of Judaism and by investing His Church
with the authority to "bind and loose" in spiritual
matters, He gave the Church warrant for celebrating
the yearly feasts, which recall the mysteries of His life.

If We Don't Remember, We Forget

As we've already mentioned, the Jewish feasts
recalled the mysteries of God's saving action among
His chosen people. God's command to celebrate
memorial feasts of this kind acknowledge an important
psychological principle. Stated simply, (and please forgive the apparent tautology) when we don't remember
God and what He has done for us, we tend to forget
Him. Whenever Israel became lax in observing God's
ritual commands, she tended to forget altogether the
covenant with Him. For example, at the time of the
sweeping religious reforms of King Josiah in the
seventh century BC, as the author of 2 Kings notes,
"[N]o such passover had been kept since the days of
the judges who judged Israel, or during all the days of
the kings of Israel or of the kings of Judah" (2 Kings
23:22). So, in direct opposition to God's command
in Exodus 12 and Leviticus 23 that the Passover be
kept as the principal yearly memorial feast of God's

saving work, there had been no such official celebration of it for four centuries!

During that same period, the kings of Israel and Judah consented to or directly engaged in horrendous acts of idolatry, including ritualized sexual misconduct, and even child sacrifice. It was this continual and wanton disregard of the covenant, caused by the disregard of the covenant liturgy, that had occasioned the reforms of King Josiah. And despite Josiah's best efforts to draw the southern kingdom of Judah back to covenantal fidelity, it would eventually lead to the return of Israel to exile, this time in Babylon rather than Egypt, beginning in 586 BC. It was almost as if God had said to the Jews, "If you won't ritually recall the last time I saved you from exile, I'll just have to exile and save you again to refresh your memory." In this respect, we are no different than our Jewish brothers and sisters; if we stop celebrating the liturgy, we will tend to forget Him.

So it is no surprise that when Jesus fulfills and perfects the Passover, He commands, "Do this in memory of me," to ensure that by liturgical recollection of His salvation of us, we will be moved to covenantal fidelity.

Time for Liturgy

God wrote the need to recall Him and His words into our human nature, and He feeds that need by commanding us to memorialize His saving work in acts of worship. This psychological principle is even suggested in the creation account. When God sets the lights in the firmament on the fourth day of creation, we are told that He does this so that they might serve "for signs and for seasons" (Gen. 1:14

RSV). Other translations render this as to "mark the fixed times" (NAB) or to "indicate festivals" (NJB). The Hebrew root term *mowed* refers to appointed times of worship and immediately suggests to Jewish ears a time of a specifically religious assembly for liturgical purposes. It is this very same word that is used in Leviticus 23:2 where God commands that the seven feasts be kept at the "time appointed." (The New American Bible suggests the liturgical connotation of *mowed* by translating the same passage with "you shall celebrate with a sacred assembly.")[8]

The biblical view of time is that its seasons and cycles are, from their creation, precisely *for* the ritual remembering that helps us remain covenantally faithful. If creation itself, and the movements of the stars and planets, are ordered to these "appointed times," then why would such festivals disappear with the advent of Christ and Christianity, as some Protestants suggest? Why would God make a world in which the cycles of time are for the regulation of worship and then end the cycle of worship before the end of time? Many denominations grudgingly recognize Easter Sunday. A few will, ironically, observe a celebration called "Reformation Sunday," but otherwise refuse to recognize the liturgical nature of time itself, as Catholics and Orthodox Christians do. While there is a growing interest in liturgy and the seasonal cycle among some Protestants, this view remains quite prominent.

As was mentioned at the beginning of this chapter, many Christians will point to a couple of verses

---

[8] See also 2 Chronicles 8:13 where the *mowadah*, the appointed festivals referred to in Leviticus 23, are observed by Solomon after the building of the Temple.

in Colossians to deny the importance of the liturgical
year: "Therefore, let no one pass judgment on you
in question of food and drink or with regard to a
festival or a new moon or a sabbath" (2:16). The
use of this text against the ancient Christian practice
of the keeping of the liturgical year ignores that it
is addressed to Christians who were likely being
encouraged to return to the *Jewish* liturgical calendar.
The next verse suggests the proper Catholic response
to those Jewish feasts: "These are only a shadow of
what is to come; but the substance belongs to Christ"
(Col. 2:17). If a shadow resembles the substance of
which is an mere reflection, that substance ought to
have the same form as it shadow.

The Letter to the Hebrews makes the same point
in reference to "what is to come." In chapter 8, we
are told that the Jewish liturgical sacrifices imparted
by Moses at the time of the Exodus "serve [as] a copy
and shadow of the heavenly sanctuary. . . . But as it is,
Christ has obtained a ministry [*leitourgia*][9] which is as
much more excellent than the old as is the covenant
he mediates is better" (Heb. 8:5–6).

In the early Church, the liturgy of Christ was
understood to be the perfect and eternal worship
that He offers before the throne of the Father on
our behalf in the mode that we see in Revelation 5:6.
There, the slain Lamb is pictured as having seven eyes,
which are identified as the seven spirits abroad on the
earth (see also 4:5). The suggestion here is that the
seven churches of Revelation 2 and 3 are immediately present with and in the liturgy that Christ presents
before the Father by means of the "the angels of the
seven churches" (1:20), who serve Christ as His very

---

[9] The Greek word from which the word "liturgy" is derived.

eyes in the world where the churches sojourn. That is, the liturgy of heaven and earth are shown to be one and the same. The twenty-four elders, who are pictured as surrounding the Lamb in His worship, suggest the twelve tribes and the twelve apostles and point to the continuity of worship from the Old Covenant to the New Covenant in Christ.

Some scholars have noted that in the New Testament there are indications not only of the liturgy of Christ, but even of the liturgical year. In 1 Corinthians 5:7–8, Saint Paul says to the Christians of that church, "For Christ, our paschal lamb, has been sacrificed. Let us, therefore, celebrate the festival, not with the old leaven, the leaven of malice and evil, but with the unleavened bread of sincerity and truth." It ought not to surprise anyone, given the centrality that Jesus Himself gave to the Passover by His celebration of the Last Supper within it, that Christians began to celebrate the same annual feast as the Jews.

And, in fact, very little time elapses in early Christian history before clear references to the annual observance of both a "Paschal Day" and the "days of Pentecost" (cf. 1 Cor. 8–9) are evident. In fact, the issue of whether to follow the practice of observing Easter on the Jewish day of Passover, 14 Nisan, or on the Sunday after, which preserves the significance of the Lord's Day of Resurrection, became one of the early sources of tension between the Eastern and Western Churches. Saint Polycarp, Bishop of Smyrna, who as a young man had been taught the Gospel by the apostle John himself, made an appeal to Pope Saint Anicetus in AD 154 in favor of the already well-established Eastern practice of celebrating on 14 Nisan. This gives witness to the fact that by this early date, in the mid-second century, in East and West, the yearly celebration of Easter was considered to be of apostolic institution.[10] The celebration of the two feasts of Easter and Pentecost remained the only universal feasts in the Church through the third century. In the fourth, Epiphany and Christmas were added, and later the feasts of the apostles and martyrs and then confessors. Eventually, in the sixth and seventh centuries, feasts of Our Lady were introduced.

This liturgical development is all contained in seed in the early celebrations of Easter, and even in the seven feasts of Judaism. Jesus came not to abolish the Old Covenant but to fulfill it; the Church, as the inheritor of His mission, has filled the year with "appointed times" that ensure we memorialize the great saving works of God in Christ. Just as Judaism had two great rounds of festivals in the first and seventh months of the year, so also the Church divides her liturgical year into two great cycles. In the late Fall and Winter, we remember the Incarnation in the Advent-Christmas-Epiphany cycle, and in the Spring and early Summer, we recall the Passion, Resurrection, Ascension, and sending of the Spirit in the Lent-Easter-Pentecost cycle. These yearly recollections serve us in just the same way that the festal cycle of the Jews served them.[11] When we don't remember Him, we for-

---

[10] Josef Jungmann, S.J., *The Early Liturgy: To the Time of Gregory the Great* (London: Dunbarton, Longman & Todd, 1963), 25–26.

[11] Other commentators have seen the Jewish feasts fulfilled in other ways. Saint Thomas Aquinas in his treatment of the ceremonial precepts of the Old Law says the following: "Passover gave place to the feast of Christ's Passion and Resurrection: the feast of Pentecost when the Old Law was given, to the feast of Pentecost on which was given the law of the living spirit: the feast of the New Moon to Lady Day, when appeared the first rays of the sun, i.e., Christ, by the fulness of grace: the feast of Trumpets, to the feasts of the Apostles: the feast of Expiation, to the feasts of the

get Him. And as Genesis and Leviticus teach, even the movements of the planets and stars have been arranged to sanctify time and so to remind us of Him who made them. For a Christian, as for an ancient Jew, time itself moves to the rhythm of liturgy.

Sean Innerst, a convert to the Catholic faith from the Religious Society of Friends (Quakers), is a seminary professor and catechist. He is a contributor to Catholic for a Reason I and II *from Emmaus Road and to Our Sunday Visitor's* Encyclopedia of Catholic Doctrine, *as well as the author of a soon-to-be published book on the sacraments. He is also preparing an adult education curriculum based on the* Catechism of the Catholic Church.

Martyrs and Confessors: the feast of Tabernacles, to the feast of the Church Dedication: the feast of Assembly and Collection, to the feast of the Angels, or else to the feast of All Hallows." *Summa Theologica* I-II, q. 103, art. 3, ad. 4.

CHAPTER VII

The Eucharist in the Apostolic Church

STEPHEN PIMENTEL

In liturgical worship, the Church re-presents the works of God. The greatest of these works revolves around His formation of the covenants by which He restores mankind to communion with Himself. These covenants form the structure of biblical history; and liturgical worship receives its form from God's eternal plan as enacted in that history. Thus, the Church "re-reads and re-lives the great events of salvation history in the 'today' of her liturgy" (*Catechism*, no. 1095). The person and work of the Messiah stand at the very heart of the liturgy as the summation of covenantal history (cf. Eph. 1:9–10), with the Great Amen of the Church ascending to the Father through Him (cf. 2 Cor. 1:20).

The apostles knew that liturgical celebration was central to their mission of extending the kingdom of God. When their preaching of the Gospel was met by intense persecution, they boldly responded, not with force of arms, but with the more powerful force of joyful thanksgiving and worship (cf. Acts 4:23–31). They had been given "power from on high" (Lk. 24:49) to restore the kingdom among mankind, and sacramental celebration was the chief means of exercising this power. Only through such celebration could the apostles fulfill their mandate to "make disciples of all nations, baptizing them in the name of the Father and of the Son and of the Holy Spirit" (Mt. 28:19).

The Eucharist, in particular, was the wellspring of their proclamation of the kingdom. At the Last Supper, Jesus had promised the apostles that they would "eat and drink at my table in my kingdom, and sit on thrones judging the twelve tribes of Israel" (Lk. 22:30). This promise is fulfilled sacramentally in the Eucharist, by which the Paschal sacrifice of the Messiah, who now reigns from heaven, is made present on earth. Leading the people of God into the presence of the King, the Eucharist is the Passover of the New Covenant.

The New Passover

In the Acts of the Apostles, the Eucharist is referred to as the "breaking of the bread." Jesus had broken bread during the Last Supper, declaring it to be "my body which is given for you" (Lk. 22:19). Likewise, He had declared the cup to be "the new covenant in my blood." In other words, His Blood is "poured out" (Lk. 22:20) to seal the New Covenant, within which the Father adopts the baptized as His sons and daughters. The Son, the Paschal Lamb (1 Cor. 5:7) whose Blood effects redemption (1 Pet. 1:18–19), is thus the covenantal mediator between the

Father and men (1 Tim. 2:5; cf. Heb. 9:14–15, 12:24).

Jesus deliberately chose the Passover as the time for the Last Supper (Lk. 22:15). The Passover commemorated the Exodus, through which God brought Israel back into covenant with Himself. Later, when the covenant was violated by idolatry, the prophets foretold a new exodus by which the Messiah would bring restoration in a new covenant (cf. Is. 52:2–6, 11–13; Jer. 31:31–32). Jesus' words at the Last Supper defined the Eucharist as the New Passover, celebrated to commemorate the New Exodus that inaugurated the New Covenant.

Jesus, "on the first day of the week" (Lk. 24:1), celebrated the Eucharist (the first Eucharist after the Last Supper) with two disciples in the village of Emmaus (Lk. 24:13, 28, 30). Hereafter, in commemoration of the Resurrection, the "first day of the week" would be a privileged time for the celebration of the Eucharist. When referring to this day (cf. Acts 20:7), Luke employs an unusual Semitism when he writes "*te de mia ton sabbaton*" (literally "on [day] one of the week"), using the cardinal *mia* (one) rather than the ordinal *prote* (first). In so doing, he follows the Septuagint's literal rendering of Genesis 1:5. This manner of expression calls to mind the creation account of Genesis 1 and points to the Eucharist as a new creation.[1]

Before celebrating the Eucharist with the two disciples at Emmaus, Jesus explained to them how His Paschal sacrifice has fulfilled "all the Scriptures" (Lk. 24:26–27). The Scriptures form a dramatic narrative

---

[1] Eugene LaVerdiere, *The Breaking of the Bread: The Development of the Eucharist According to Acts* (Chicago: Liturgy Training Publications, 1998), 94–95.

of which the mission of Christ is the climax. The disciples, however, are only able to grasp this fulfillment "in the breaking of the bread" (Lk. 24:35). The Scriptures and Communion—Liturgy of the Word and Liturgy of the Eucharist—must go together to be understood, and both are to be spread "to all nations" (Lk. 24:47).

The Breaking of the Bread

In his depiction of the apostolic Church in Jerusalem, Luke describes the disciples as "devot[ing] themselves to the apostles' teaching and fellowship, to the breaking of bread and the prayers" (Acts 2:42). Fellowship, or communion (*koinonia*), can be defined as "participation in the Mystical Body of Christ through the sacramental Body of Christ."[2] Hence, fellowship and "the breaking of bread" are inseparably linked (cf. 1 Cor. 10:16–17). Communion is brought about within the Church through Christ's Eucharistic presence. The Church rejoices in His presence through "the prayers," which consist of a liturgical service centered on the communal reading of Scripture and recitation of psalms, in the manner of the Liturgy of Hours.

As time went on, the disciples continued to obey Jesus' command at the Last Supper (Lk. 22:19) by "breaking bread" as He had taught them (Acts 2:46). They faithfully attended to the Eucharist "day by day," just as the Israelites, who ate "bread from heaven" in the wilderness, gathered "a day's portion every day" (Ex. 16:4). Luke reports that the disciples broke bread "*kat' oikon*," which is best translated "as a household." This phrase recalls the instructions for

---

[2] Stephen Pimentel, *Witnesses of the Messiah: On the Acts of the Apostles 1–15* (Steubenville, OH: Emmaus Road, 2002), 50.

the Passover feast, according to which the Israelites were to take "a lamb according to their fathers' houses [*kat' oikous*], a lamb for a household [*kat' oikian*]" (Ex. 12:3, LXX).[3] The notion of a "household," in the context of the Passover feast, was not strictly limited to a single family. When the size of the families was small, Scripture made provision for multiple families to share a lamb (Ex. 12:4). First-century Judaism interpreted this provision broadly in terms of a *habhurah*, or "company united for the celebration of the Passover."[4] Therefore, breaking bread "*kat' oikon*" refers not so much to the location of the Eucharistic celebration, as to its celebration in a company that was formed into a spiritual family through communion.[5]

During his third missionary journey, while returning to Jerusalem, Paul spent a week in Troas (Acts 20:6–12). In his description of this sojourn, Luke gives us the only narrative account in Acts of a particular celebration of the Eucharist. The disciples in Troas gather "on the first day of the week . . . to break bread" (Acts 20:7). Luke again refers literally to day "one" of the week, echoing his earlier account of Jesus' Eucharistic celebration at Emmaus. The gathering was planned for the purpose of a Eucharistic celebration, suggesting that such liturgies had already become customary on Sundays. During the first part of the liturgy, Paul, knowing that he would never again visit Troas, gave an unusually long sermon (Acts 20:7). When

[3] Eugenio Zolli, *The Nazarene*, trans. Cyril Vollert (New Hope, KY: Urbi et Orbi/Remnant of Israel, 1999), 202.

[4] David Daube, *The New Testament and Rabbinic Judaism* (Peabody, MA: Hendrickson, 1956), 332. As an example, Daube notes (in footnote 3) that, where Exodus 12:46 states that the Passover feast should be eaten "in one house," several of the Targums read "in one habhurah."

[5] Zolli, 203.

the time for the consecration came, it was Paul himself who "broke the bread" (Acts 20:11), highlighting the role of the individual ministerial priesthood. After the Eucharistic celebration, Paul "conversed" [*homilesas*] with the congregation. A *homilia* is a company gathered for fellowship,[6] reminiscent of the Passover *habhura*. Luke's language frames the Eucharistic congregation as a company united in communion through the New Passover celebration.

The Wilderness Generation

In his own writings, Paul, even more than Luke, develops an understanding of the Eucharist as the Messianic fulfillment of the Passover (1 Cor. 5:7). In fact, he presents a subtle typology in which both Baptism and the Eucharist are seen as the disciple's participation in the New Exodus, bringing the disciple, not into the land of Canaan, but into the Body of Christ. This typology centers on the generation of Israelites who were led out of Egypt in the Exodus and, thereafter, wandered for forty years in the wilderness. Paul explains that the experiences of these Israelites can be seen as "types" (*typikos*) for the instruction of the disciple living at the end of the Deuteronomic covenant (1 Cor. 10:6, 11).[7] Such typology is not merely a literary device or metaphor, but rather, reflects a pattern that God has imprinted on history as part of His salvific economy. Paul refers to the Israelites of the wilderness generation as the "fathers" of his Gentile converts (1 Cor. 10:1), not because of their ancestry, but because, through Baptism, the latter have been

---

[6] LaVerdiere, 212.
[7] Richard B. Hays, *Echoes of Scripture in the Letters of Paul* (New Haven, CT: Yale University Press, 1989), 91.

incorporated into the restored Israel. According to
Paul's typology, the cloud of glory (cf. Ex. 13:21) corresponds to the Holy Spirit, and the passage through
the Red Sea to the water of Baptism (1 Cor. 10:2).
Likewise, the manna in the wilderness corresponds to
the Eucharistic Body of Christ (1 Cor. 10:3), and the
water from the rock to His Eucharistic Blood (1 Cor.
10:4).

Water from the rock was miraculously given to
the Israelites on two occasions. On the first occasion,
Moses struck the rock with his rod (Ex. 17:3–6). The
second occurred toward the end of the forty years of
wandering, as the Israelites were preparing to enter
Canaan (Num. 20:2–13). On this occasion, God told
Moses and Aaron only to speak to the rock in order to
elicit the miraculous water. Moses, however, did not
obey. Apparently he could not believe that the water
would come forth simply through the mere speaking
of words. Instead, he desired something that could be
seen, and so, in disobedience, he struck the rock. By
his act of unbelief, Moses, in the presence of the people of Israel, failed to treat God as holy (Num. 20:12).
The holiness of God is honored through faithful
obedience, trusting in His word even when one does
not yet see its fulfillment. God's plan had been for
the rock to be struck only once, and thereafter it was
to bring forth the miraculous drink when spoken to.[8]
Paul identifies the rock with Christ (1 Cor. 10:4), who
brings forth the miraculous drink, His Eucharistic
Blood, when spoken to by God's appointed priest.

In developing his Eucharistic typology, Paul does
not limit his exposition to the allegorical sense of

[8] Rev. Michael Duggan, *The Consuming Fire: A Christian Introduction to the Old Testament* (San Francisco: Ignatius Press, 1991), 129–30.

Israelite history, but also explores its moral sense (cf. Catechism, no. 117), delving into the ethical implications of that history for the baptized. Paul quotes from the account of the golden calf (Ex. 32:6; 1 Cor. 10:7), employing his Eucharistic typology to invoke the memory of the Israelites' idolatry and immorality as a warning to New Covenant disciples against analogous sins. The beginning of the quotation, "the people sat down to eat and drink," follows Paul's exposition of the Israelites' spiritual eating and drinking. The end of the quotation, "and rose up to dance," precedes his description of the sins into which the Israelites nevertheless fell (1 Cor. 10:8–10). Thus, the Israelites' spiritual eating and drinking, though types of the Eucharist, did not prevent them from falling into idolatry and immorality.[9] Paul, therefore, warns the disciples against such sins, which destroy the unity with the Body of Christ that is established in the Eucharist.

Paul describes the Eucharistic cup as the "cup of blessing," employing the phrase that is used for the third cup of the Passover supper (1 Cor. 10:16). As a participation in the Body and Blood of Christ, the New Passover is a true sacrifice, one in which an uncreated Person offers Himself as a sacrifice which surpasses all other sacrifices. The Eucharistic cult must, therefore, overthrow the cult of every other deity, not only in exterior worship, but also in one's interior disposition. Worship given to any created reality, however great, is idolatry and ultimately demonic in inspiration (cf. 1 Cor. 10:21).

Those who participate in the New Passover are the members of the restored Israel, the "one Body"

---

[9] Hays, 92.

of Christ (1 Cor. 10:17).[10] The establishment of such union within the Body of Christ is the true significance of the *koinonia* practiced in the breaking of the bread. Thus, the one people of God is brought into being by the Eucharist, for "*the Eucharist makes the Church*" (*Catechism*, no. 1396, italics in original). The disciple is united to Christ the Head and, through Him, to the other disciples, "a transformation from glory to glory" (2 Cor. 3:18, cf. *EE* 23).[11]

The doctrine of the Eucharist rests on the words of Christ at the Last Supper, which Paul "received" and "delivered [*paredoka*]" as Sacred Tradition [*paradosis*] (1 Cor. 11:23). According to this Tradition, Christ pronounced the Eucharistic cup to be "the new covenant in my blood" (1 Cor. 11:25), referring to Jeremiah's prophecy of covenantal restoration for Israel (Jer. 31:31–33). In uttering these words over the cup, Jesus declared that His ministry was reaching its culmination in the ratification of the New Covenant. Thereafter, those who share in the Eucharist would be the people of God restored in that covenant.

Christ further instructed His disciples to celebrate the Eucharist "in remembrance [*anamnesis*] of me" (1 Cor. 11:24) so as to renew the covenant He had established. The Eucharist is not merely a subjective remembering of Christ's death and Resurrection but a sacred *anamnesis* of those events (1 Cor. 11:26), a covenantal renewal that makes really present His Body and Blood. Therefore, to partake of Communion unworthily is to make oneself guilty of sacrilege (cf. 1 Cor. 11:27–29; *EE* 12, 36).

---

[10] N. T. Wright, *What Saint Paul Really Said: Was Paul of Tarsus the Real Founder of Christianity?* (Grand Rapids: Wm. B. Eerdmans, 1997), 87.

[11] See also Matthias Joseph Scheeben, *The Mysteries of Christianity*, trans. Cyril Vollert, S.J. (St. Louis: B. Herder, 1946), 502, 533.

The Heavenly Tabernacle

In the Epistle to the Hebrews, the importance of the covenantal dimension of the Eucharist for the apostolic Church is brought out even more forcefully. Jesus is described as the High Priest (Heb. 6:20) who guarantees "a better covenant" (Heb. 7:22) than the Deuteronomic covenant which was passing away (Heb. 7:18–19). Now that God has ratified the New Covenant "with an oath" (Heb. 7:21), the disciples are always able to "draw near" in the liturgy to Christ's Paschal sacrifice (Heb. 7:19). From the time of His Exaltation onward, Christ's sacrifice remains perpetually before the Father (Heb. 7:24–27). Christ serves as our minister (*leitourgos*) in the heavenly tabernacle (Heb. 8:2), offering His physical Body—no longer bloody, but glorified—for His Mystical Body, the Church (Heb. 8:3). The Church, in turn, participates in this unbloody sacrifice in the Eucharist. Thus, the Eucharistic liturgy (*leitourgia*) is "public worship" performed by Christ the Head in heaven and by His Body on earth (*Catechism*, no. 1070). Because of its heavenly nature, the liturgy of the New Covenant is "much more excellent" than that of the Mosaic covenant (Heb. 8:6). Indeed, in light of the New Covenant, the Mosaic covenant is seen to be "obsolete" (Heb. 8:13), for its sacrifices were bound to the earthly Temple and could not be offered in the heavenly one (Heb. 9:8–10).

Christ's sacrifice culminates in His new Exodus, by which He has entered into the "greater and more perfect" tabernacle "not made with hands" (Heb. 9:11) to offer His own Blood for "an eternal redemption" (Heb. 9:12). His sacrifice is grounded in earthly history, but not bound within its confines.

Rather, it ascends into the heavenly realm, making possible the sacramental identity of Eucharist and Crucifixion. The Eucharistic celebration is thus the nexus between heaven and earth, wherein Christ is present under the appearance of bread and wine, just as in heaven He is present in His glorified humanity. By His sacrifice, "the heavens have been opened," allowing the Eucharistic liturgy to be celebrated on earth.[12] As Christ offered Himself to the Father through the Spirit, so He now offers "the blood of the eternal covenant" to sanctify the disciple (Heb. 9:14; 13:20).[13] We are not bereft of Christ's heavenly gift, for "we have an altar" (Heb. 13:10) from which we receive "everything good" (Heb. 13:21).

Christ invites us to follow Him into the heavenly tabernacle through His own Body and Blood. In the Eucharist, the Kingdom of God is extended from heaven into our bodies and souls, allowing us in turn to enter the presence of the Father. The sacrifice of Christ on Calvary was an historical event that objectively effected the Redemption. The Ascension did not remove it from history. Rather, the Ascension brings the sacrifice before the Father and makes possible Christ's Exaltation, in which the Spirit extends the sacrifice throughout history. The Eucharist thus participates in the interchange of Trinitarian gifts: the Word uttered by the Father offers Himself back to the Father through the Spirit. This interchange takes place first in eternity, then on Calvary, then

---

[12] Joseph Cardinal Ratzinger, *A New Song for the Lord: Faith in Christ and Liturgy Today*, trans. Martha M. Matesich (New York: A Crossroad Herder Book, Crossroad, 1997), 133.
[13] Scheeben, 519.

in the heavenly Temple, and finally in the Eucharist throughout time.

Stephen Pimentel is the author of Witnesses of the Messiah: On Acts of the Apostles 1–15 *(Emmaus Road) and a contributor to* Lay Witness *magazine. He holds an M.A. in theology from Christendom College.*

CHAPTER VIII

The Mass and the Apocalypse

MICHAEL BARBER

The Book of Revelation sits in the back of many people's Bibles as an enigma, an un-crack-able code. In fact, Martin Luther considered throwing the book out of the Bible altogether—and he was not the first to attempt to do so. Left scratching their heads, most Catholics like to leave it for the more familiar territory of the Gospels or the Psalms. What comes as a shock to many Catholics is this: the Apocalypse describes the one thing that Catholics are *most* familiar with—the Mass.

We have all heard wild theories about the Book of Revelation. Jehovah's Witnesses explain that it foretells the day the entire planet Earth will be transformed into a type of paradise, a new Garden of Eden where all believers—except the 144,000 in Heaven (cf. Rev. 14:1)—will live forever. Some Protestants, like Jerry Falwell, believe that it describes a time in the future where Christ will return to live on earth for a thousand years, reigning as King in a newly built Jerusalem Temple. Other interpretations focus on the identity of the dragon, the beast or the meaning of his infamous number, "666."

Usually, proponents of these theories will try to convince you that Revelation is being fulfilled in the headlines of the day's newspapers. For example, they might point out that modern Iraq was once the place where ancient Babylon stood and then try to interpret today's events in light of the Book of Revelation. This is nothing new. In the nineteen-eighties, Hal Lindsey in his best-selling book, *The Late Great Planet Earth*, claimed that the Red Dragon described in Revelation 12 symbolized "red" China. Even further back in history, preachers in the Old West insisted that the Indians were to be seen as the coming of the evil horsemen described in Revelation 9:17.[1]

All of these interpretations are centered on aspects of the Apocalypse—the 144,000, the Millennium, the dragon, the beast, 666, etc. In this short article, it is not possible to comment fully on the relevance of these texts.[2] Yet, it is noteworthy that none of these images occur more than a couple of times in the Apocalypse. The dragon and the beast are not mentioned until the middle of the book and are only mentioned a few times afterwards (Rev. 12; 13; 16; 20). The 144,000 are not mentioned until chapter 7 (Rev. 7:4) and are only mentioned again in chapter fourteen (Rev. 14:1). The Millennium appears only once, at the very end of the book (Rev. 20:3; 7). The number of the beast, "666," also occurs only one time (Rev. 13:18).

---

[1] J. L. Martin, *The Voice of the Seven Thunders* (Bedford, IN: James M. Mathes, 1873), 151ff.

[2] See my *Coming Soon: Unlocking the Book of Revelation and Applying Its Lessons Today*, (Emmaus Road) due to be published in 2004.

Sooner or Later

Sensationalistic theories may sell a lot of books, but they fail to explain the true theme of the Book of Revelation. A closer look at the Book of Revelation is clearly needed. The beast is not the theme of the book, nor is the Millennium, nor any of the other cryptic images.

What is the dominant message of the Apocalypse? From the opening verses to the very last chapter, Jesus insists that He is "coming soon" (for example, Rev. 1:1; 22:20). Jesus' coming is *the* message. Furthermore, throughout the book there is another major motif wrapped up tightly with Jesus' coming. Unlike the other images mentioned above, it is found throughout every chapter—that is, the liturgy.

In *The Lamb's Supper*, Scott Hahn points out a few of the familiar elements from the Mass that are found in the Book of Revelation.

—Sunday worship	1:10
—a high priest	1:13
—an altar	8:3–4; 11:1;14:18
—priests (*"presbyteroi"*)	4:4; 11:16; 14:3; 19:4
—vestments	1:13; 4:4; 6:11; 7:9; 15:6; 19:13–14
—consecrated celibacy	14:4
—men in white robes	4:4
—the tabernacle (tent)	15:5
—lampstands (Menorah)	1:12; 2:5
—incense	5:8; 8:3–5
—chalices	15:7; 16:1; 21:9
—the Sign of the Cross (*"tau"*)	7:3; 14:1; 22:4
—the Gloria	15:3–4
—the Alleluia	19:1, 3, 4, 6,

—Lift up your hearts	11:12
—the Holy, Holy, Holy	4:8
—the Amen	19:4; 22:21
—the Lamb of God	5:6 and throughout
—intercession of angels and saints	5:8; 6:9–10; 8:3–4
—antiphonal chant	4:8–11; 5:9–14; 7:10–12; 18:1–8
—silent contemplation	8:1
—kneeling before Christ	1:17; 4:10
—God's faithful singing praise	4:8; 5:9; 14:3; 15:3
—the marriage supper of the Lamb	19:9, cf. 19:17[3]

Only in the context of the liturgy can we make sense out of the Apocalypse.

These liturgical elements are not simply mentioned in passing, nor are they haphazardly tacked on to John's visions. The Book of Revelation describes the events on earth as unfolding according to the prayers of the saints offered in the heavenly liturgy. In fact, whether it is the opening of a seal or a half hour of silence, everything that happens on earth occurs because something has been enacted in the heavenly liturgy. As the people of God celebrate the liturgy, the very course of history is affected.[4]

---

[3] Adapted from Scott Hahn, *The Lamb's Supper* (New York: Doubleday, 1999), 119–20.

[4] Leonard Thompson, a non-Catholic scholar, observes, "Even a cursory reading of the Book of Revelation shows the presence of liturgical language set in worship. Moreover, as we shall see, the language of worship plays an important role in unifying the book, that is, in making it a coherent apocalypse in both form and content. The scenes of worship are not just 'interludes' or 'interruptions' in the dramatic narration of eschatology; they take their place alongside these narrations of eschatology to make of the book something more than visions of 'things to come.'" *The Book of Revelation: Apocalypse and Empire* (New York: Oxford University Press, 1990), 53.

The *Catechism of the Catholic Church* makes the connection between the Mass and the Apocalypse clear when it teaches, "The book of *Revelation* of St. John, read in the Church's liturgy, first reveals to us, 'A throne stood in heaven, with one seated on the throne': 'the Lord God' [Rev. 4:2, 8; Is. 6:1; cf. Ezek. 1:26–28]. It then shows the Lamb, 'standing as though it had been slain' [Rev. 5:6; *Liturgy of St. John Chrysostom*, Anaphora; cf. Jn. 1:29; Heb. 4:14–15; 10:19–2]: Christ crucified and risen, the one high priest of the true sanctuary, the same one 'who offers and is offered, who gives and is given.' Finally, it presents the 'river of the water of life . . . flowing from the throne of God and of the Lamb,' one of the most beautiful symbols of the Holy Spirit [Rev. 22:1, cf. 21:6, Jn. 4:10–14]" (no. 1137).

In other words, the Book of Revelation can only be properly understood when it is read in the light of the Church's liturgy. There we enter into the spiritual realities described in the Apocalypse. In the liturgy, we affect history as the saints do in Revelation. However, without the liturgy, John's vision is simply confusing, and history becomes quite frightening.

Half-ing to Do with the Liturgy

The connection between the liturgy and the Apocalypse may also be seen in the way the two are structured. Scholars note that the Book of Revelation can be divided neatly into two parts, Revelation 1–11 and Revelation 12–22. In the first half, the focus is a book with seven seals, which must be opened and read. The second half describes seven chalices that are poured out, climaxing in the marriage supper where the Lamb is united to the Bride.

This parallels the structure of the Mass. The first part of the Mass is the Liturgy of the Word, which revolves around the reading of the book—the Bible. The second part is the Liturgy of the Eucharist, where the Church, the Bride of Christ, receives the Lamb of God, in the chalice.

In addition, prior to the opening of the book with seven seals, Revelation begins with letters to the seven churches, which call for repentance. Similarly, the Mass begins with the Penitential Rite, in which we confess our sins and ask the Lord for mercy and forgiveness. Only after doing this do we proceed to the Scripture readings.

Liturgical from the Start

From the opening verses of the book, it is clear that the Church's liturgy is the proper context for the Apocalypse. "Blessed is he who reads aloud the words of the prophecy, and blessed are those who hear" (Rev. 1:3). The "one who reads" is the lector and "those who hear" refer to the congregation.

Next, John sets the stage for his vision. He tells us both where he was and what he was doing when he received his vision. "I was in the Spirit on the Lord's Day" (Rev. 1:10). This term, "the Lord's Day," was universally used in the early Church to refer to Sunday, the day commemorating the Resurrection (cf. *Catechism*, nos. 2174–75). Of course, it was also the day the Church celebrated the Eucharist. Only, on this particular Sunday, John is going to Mass, not in his local parish where He celebrated the liturgy as Bishop, but in heaven, where Christ reigns as High Priest.

In the vision, John finds himself in the presence

of seven lampstands. "Then I turned to see the voice that was speaking to me, and on turning I saw seven golden lampstands" (Rev. 1:12). These seven lampstands symbolize the special candelabra known as the "menorah," such as those used in the celebration of the Jewish feast of Chanukah. The menorah was located in the Temple and was cared for by the priests.

The next thing John sees is Jesus dressed as a High Priest: "I saw seven lampstands and in the midst of the seven lampstands one like a son of man, clothed with a long robe and with a golden girdle round his breast" (Rev. 1:12–13). Chapter one of the Book of Revelation thus gives us the context for the visions found in the remainder of the book by placing us in the heavenly Temple with the heavenly High Priest. From the beginning, John uses the liturgy as the setting for the Book of Revelation.

Dinner Invitations

Throughout the rest of the Apocalypse, liturgical and Eucharistic references abound. In the letter to the church of Pergamum, Jesus says, "To him who conquers I will give some of the hidden manna" (Rev. 2:17). Tradition tells us that the Book of Revelation was written by the same person who wrote the Fourth Gospel, the Apostle John.[5] In the sixth chapter of that Gospel, Jesus tells us what the true manna is, "Your fathers ate the manna in the wilderness, and they died. . . . I am the living bread which came down from heaven; if any one eats of this bread he will live for ever; and the bread which

---

[5] Many scholars today are skeptical that John actually wrote Revelation. For a defense of his authorship, see my *Coming Soon: Unlocking the Book of Revelation and Applying Its Lessons Today* (Steubenville, OH: Emmaus Road).

I will give for the life of the world is my flesh" (6:49, 51). Veiled behind the appearances of bread and wine, Jesus comes to us in the Eucharist as the "hidden manna."

At the end of the seven letters, Jesus says, "Behold, I stand at the door and knock; if any one hears my voice and opens the door, I will come in to him and eat with him, and he with me" (Rev. 3:20). Even non-Catholic scholars recognize this as a reference to the Eucharist.[6]

Coming Up

After writing down the letters to the seven churches as dictated by Jesus, John has another vision. John sees an open door to heaven and hears a voice saying, "Come up!" (Rev. 4:1). Instantly, John finds himself in the throne room of heaven. There he sees twenty-four "elders" (Rev. 4:4). The Greek word for "elders" is *presbyters*, from which we get the English word "priest." These presbyters wear white robes and join with the angels singing a hymn Catholics will immediately recognize—"Holy, holy, holy" (Rev. 4:8). While they are singing, incense is offered to God with the prayers of the saints (Rev. 5:8).

From this we learn where we really are when we are at Mass—we are in heaven. This far surpasses

---

[6] In his commentary on this passage, one of these non-Catholic scholars, David Chilton, writes, "We must take seriously the Biblical doctrine of the Real Presence of Christ in the sacrament of the Eucharist. We must return to the Biblical pattern of worship centered on Jesus Christ, which means the weekly celebration of the Lord's Supper, as well as instruction about its true meaning. . . . In Holy Communion we are genuinely having dinner with Jesus, lifted up into His heavenly presence; and, moreover, we are feasting on Him." *The Days of Vengeance: An Exposition of the Book of Revelation* (Fort Worth, TX: Dominion Press, 1987), 138.

what was realized in the Old Covenant worship. Ancient Israel knew that there was a liturgy in heaven, but they could only take comfort in knowing that their Temple worship mirrored the worship of the angels in heaven.

In the Mass, we are not merely *imitating* the heavenly liturgy—we are *participating* in it. As revealed in the Apocalypse, when we sing, "Holy, holy, holy," we sing with the angels and saints in heaven. "[The Eucharist] unites heaven and earth" (*EE* 8). This is why the priest reminds us, "Lift up your hearts." We are joining in the heavenly chorus. When we go to Mass, we go to heaven. All our patron saints, our guardian angels, and our loved ones already in heaven surround us in the Mass.

Agnus Dei

In Revelation 5, John sees a scroll with writing on both sides.[7] This scroll is sealed with seven seals. No one, however, is worthy to break the seals and open the scroll. The scroll represents the Old Covenant. The Hebrew word for "seven" is also the word used for "swearing" a covenant oath. In Hebrew, to swear an oath literally means "to seven oneself."

The saints and angels weep because no one is found worthy to open the scrolls and so fulfill God's covenant promises. John is then told that he is about to behold the conquering Messiah, the "Lion of the Tribe of Judah"—the one who is worthy to open the seven seals (Rev. 5:5). But instead of a triumphant lion, John sees Jesus as a "Lamb standing, as though it had been slain" (Rev. 5:6).

---

[7] In fact, other covenant documents, e.g. the Ten Commandments, were also written on both sides (Ex. 32:15).

Slain lambs, of course, cannot stand. Once dead, they slump and fall over. But Jesus the "slain Lamb" is "standing," as the resurrected Messiah. The point is clear—Jesus has conquered through His self-offering. He stands before the Father in heaven forever, re-presenting Himself as the one true sacrifice for sin.

From chapter 5 through the end of the book—in all, 17 chapters—Jesus is called the "Lamb" twenty-eight times. No other title even qualifies for a close second. Not surprisingly, the title used most often to describe Jesus underscores the role He plays in the heavenly liturgy. Not only is He High Priest, He is also the sacrificial victim of the New Passover.

The New Passover

In the first Passover, God delivered Israel from the bondage of slavery and led them out of Egypt to the Promised Land. The Passover consisted of three elements. First, an unblemished lamb was to be sacrificed. Next, each family was to take the blood of the lamb and sprinkle their houses with it. Once this was complete, the family was to eat the lamb.

As the New Passover Lamb, Christ was sacrificed and His Blood was shed; yet something more is still necessary. As Israel ate the lamb, we too must we eat the Body and Blood of Christ. Paul makes this point when he says, "Christ our Passover Lamb has been sacrificed. Let us, therefore, keep the feast" (1 Cor. 5:7–8). Jesus began to prepare the Apostles for this teaching during His next to last Passover on earth, insisting, "Truly, truly, I say to you, unless you eat the flesh of the Son of man and drink His blood, you have no life in you; . . . For my flesh is food indeed and my blood is drink indeed." (Jn. 6:53, 55).

On the night Israel celebrated the old Passover, Jesus instituted the Eucharist, the Passover of the New Covenant. In the old Passover, Israel commemorated the day that the Lord delivered them from slavery and began to lead them to the Promised Land. In the New Passover, Christ delivers us from true slavery, bondage to sin, and brings us into the true Promised Land, Heaven. This is what is described in the Book of Revelation.

For example, in Revelation 15 the saints who have passed through the tribulation and entered into heaven are portrayed as standing by a fiery red sea, singing, "the song of Moses" (Rev. 15:2–3). They are like the Israelites who stood on the other side of the Red Sea, praising God for delivering them from the charioteers of the Egyptians. The saints celebrate the New Passover in the climactic vision at the end of the Apocalypse—the Marriage Supper of the Lamb.

Alleluia!!!

As we have already said, when Jesus ate His Last Supper, He was celebrating a Passover meal. In ancient Israel, the Passover was celebrated as an elaborate seder meal, which involved four cups and the singing of the Hallel Psalms (Psalms 113–118). "Hallel," means "praise." It is from this word that we get our English word, "Hallelujah" or "Alleluia." "Yah," the short form in Hebrew for God's name ("Yahweh") when combined with Hallel means, "praise God."

After the persecutors of God's people are judged in Revelation 17–18, John sees the angels and saints at a meal celebrated in the heavenly Mount Zion, where they sing "Hallelujah!" Just as the Passover meal was celebrated with the drinking of the seder cups and

the singing of the "Hallel" Psalms, Revelation depicts
a meal that is celebrated after the "cups" are poured
out (Rev. 16–17) and after the saints sing "Hallelujah"
(Rev. 19:1–9). John thus sees the Eucharist as the New
Passover celebrated in the heavenly Promised Land.

The Second Vatican Council taught, "In the
earthly liturgy we take part in a foretaste of that
heavenly liturgy which is celebrated in the holy city
of Jerusalem toward which we journey as pilgrims"
(*SC* 8). When we go to Mass we truly enter into
heaven, in the Eucharist, we truly enter into communion with the Divine Trinity. However, we are
reminded that we are not yet there. As Israel wandered in the desert before entering into the Promised
Land, we journey through this life as pilgrims on our
way to our heavenly homeland. Just as Israel received
manna from heaven, we receive the hidden manna as
our spiritual food. Through the Eucharistic banquet,
the Passover Feast, we learn to offer up our trials and
sufferings and so prepare to enter fully into the life of
the Trinity in heaven.

Called to His Supper

At the end of the Book of Revelation, John has
a vision of the New Jerusalem—the heavenly city.
However, this Jerusalem is different than the Old
Jerusalem, since it is missing the one thing that made
the old city so important—the Temple. "And I saw no
temple in the city, for its temple is the Lord God the
Almighty and the Lamb" (Rev. 21:22). In the New
Jerusalem, we live forever in the true Temple, which is
God Himself.

Heaven, the *Catechism* teaches, is entering into
God's life (cf. *Catechism*, no. 1024). God's life is noth-

ing less than the self-giving love shared by the Trinity. The Father pours Himself out into the Son in love, the Son images the Father by pouring Himself back out to the Father in love, and this love that they share is the Holy Spirit.

In Mass we enter into communion with this Divine Trinity. We are called to pour ourselves out in love by offering up our lives, all that we have, and all that we are. We find ourselves, like John, in the Spirit on the Lord's day, and we hear that wondrous invitation—the greatest dinner invitation of them all—"Come up!"

Michael Barber is the author of a verse by verse commentary on the Book of Revelation, Coming Soon: Unlocking the Apocalypse and Applying Its Lessons Today, *(Emmaus Road), and* Singing in the Reign: The Psalms and the Liturgy of God's Kingdom *(Emmaus Road). He holds a master's degree in theology from Franciscan University of Steubenville.*

CHAPTER IX

The Difference
Jesus Makes
*The Eucharist and
Christian Living*

LEON J. SUPRENANT, JR.

At Mass, we encounter the mystery of Christ becoming truly present under the appearance of bread and wine. Even though the sacred species look exactly the same after the consecration as they did before the consecration, we know by faith that there's a world of difference. Our Lord and Savior is truly present in our midst as our spiritual food. The change could not be more dramatic, nor more imperceptible.

That's the objective reality of what we call transubstantiation. But what does our encounter with this mystery actually do to *us*? In other words, what about those of us who are standing in line for Holy Communion? Do we look any different as we walk back to our pews? After all, the Body and Blood of Jesus Christ are inside us. Are we any different fifteen minutes later, in the church parking lot or in the parish hall? Are we any different two or three days later? As we consider this issue, we quickly discover that the mystery of the Eucharist leads inexorably to the mystery of the Church and Christian living, just as the mystery of the objective redemption of humanity leads to a consideration of our own redemption.

From the first Christians, who gathered for the "breaking of the bread" (Acts 2:46), to parishes today, which Pope John Paul II calls "Eucharistic communities,"[1] the Eucharist has always been an integral part of Christian living. Through the regenerative waters of Baptism, the baptized have become "new creations" (2 Cor. 5:17)—that is, Christian. Furthermore, Christians are exhorted not to return to their old ways, but rather to change further—to become more conformed to Christ (cf. Eph. 4:17–24). This internal transformation is real, but not always perceptible. Saint Peter says: "Once you were no people but now you are God's people" (1 Pet. 2:10). Do "God's people" look different from "no people"? If so, how? And what role does the Eucharist play in this continual gathering and transforming of the human family into God's own family?

Effectively living what we celebrate at Mass has always been a central concern of the Church, and certainly that's true in our own day. Regardless of what one might think of the liturgical reforms ushered in by Vatican II (1962–65), or of liturgy in general, it is indisputably true that liturgical vitality is a primary concern of the Church.

The first words of the first document issued by Vatican II are: "The sacred Council . . . desires to impart an ever increasing vigor to the Christian life

---

[1] Pope John Paul II, Apostolic Exhortation *Christifideles Laici* (December 30, 1988), no. 26.

of the faithful" (*SC* 1). A couple lines further down, the document says that it is in the sacred liturgy, especially the Eucharist, where "the faithful may express in their lives, and manifest to others, the mystery of Christ and the real nature of the true Church" (*SC* 2).

How does the Eucharist empower us to live more effective, "vigorous" Christian lives? In answering this question, let's reflect on a few biblical passages that shed light on different aspects of this complex topic.

"I Am the Way and the Truth and the Life" (Jn. 14:6)

It should be self-evident that Christ is the center of Christian living. After all, there is no salvation in any one else (cf. Acts 4:12), and at the heart of the Gospel is the clarion call to follow Jesus, to become His disciples (e.g., Lk. 9:23).

Those of us who have heard and accepted our Lord's summons to follow Him are invited to an intimate, personal relationship with Him. Unfortunately, some Catholics may be put off by this "personal relationship" terminology. Yet, Christianity is not a mere moral code, ethnic club, or cultural phenomenon; rather, at its very core is the acceptance of Jesus Christ, the Son of God, as our personal Lord and Savior.

Such a relationship with our Lord necessarily entails a network of ecclesial, familial relationships. Those of us who come from large families (I'm the youngest of fourteen children) know firsthand how families can mushroom to such an extent that we can barely keep track of all our relatives. Yet, the reason we have these relationships at all is that we were born into the same family, that we share a common father.

Similarly, our relationship with Jesus Christ is such
that He empowers us to be children of God—His
brothers and sisters by adoption (cf. Rom. 8:14–15).

So we have a relationship with our Lord that is
both personal and familial. We also know that this
relationship must be central in our lives. If a husband ignores his spouse, his marriage will suffer. If
someone never communicates with her best friend,
they will stop being best friends. Similarly, our Lord
expects our full commitment to this relationship with
Him. That is why in Scripture He harshly condemns
indifference or tepidity: "I know your works: you
are neither cold nor hot. Would that you were cold
or hot! So, because you are lukewarm, and neither
cold nor hot, I will spew you out of my mouth" (Rev.
3:15–16).

But how do we *live* our personal relationship
with Jesus Christ? We reach for Him, knowing that
He is present to us in many ways. At anytime, we can
call upon Him in prayer. He is present in His Word,
which is "living and active" (Heb. 4:12). He is present where two or three are gathered in His name
(cf. Mt. 18:20). He is present in the person of His
apostles and their successors—namely, the Pope and
bishops—such that those who hear them hear Christ
(Lk. 10:16). He is present in the poor and forgot-
ten in our midst (cf. Mt. 25:34–40). All these and
other ways of encountering Christ and nourishing
our personal relationship with Him are legitimate
and extremely important. But beyond these, we
encounter Christ most fully, most intimately—Body,
Blood, Soul, and Divinity—in the Eucharist. We say
that He is most especially present in the Eucharist
because such presence is not only spiritual, but tan-

gible and corporeal (cf. *Catechism*, no. 1374). Jesus is the "life," and when we bodily receive our Lord, the "living bread," in the Eucharist, we truly partake of and draw upon this supernatural source of life (Jn. 6:51).

"[T]he Eucharistic sacrifice is the source and the summit of the whole of the Church's worship and of the Christian life."[2] This synthesis of Vatican II's teaching helps to put this issue in sharper focus. The Eucharist is the *summit* of Christian living. And "summit" assumes an upward orientation. To appreciate the "summit" most fully, we need to order our lives around the Eucharist, to ensure we are properly disposed to worthily receive the Sacrament. While weekly Mass is the "minimum," more frequent participation is warmly encouraged by the Church, as is Eucharistic adoration outside of Mass (cf. *EE* 25).

The Eucharist is also the *source* of Christian living. As Jesus Himself says, "[A]part from me you can do nothing" (Jn. 15:5). Nothing. Nada. Zilch. Each moment a living branch draws nutrients and life itself from the vine. Similarly, through the Eucharist, Jesus continually communicates to us His grace which is nothing less than the nutrients we need to sustain us in our daily Christian discipleship (cf. Jn. 15:1–6).

"You Did Not Choose Me, but I Chose You" (Jn. 15:16)

Even as we recognize the need for a personal relationship with our Lord and for nurturing this

---

[2] Sacred Congregation of Rites, Instruction on the Worship of the Eucharistic Mystery *Eucharisticum Mysterium* (1967), no. 3(e), in Austin Flannery, O.P., ed, *Vatican Council II*, vol. 1, *The Conciliar and Post Conciliar Documents*, new rev. ed. (Northport, NY: Costello, 1996), 104.

relationship, we must continually return to this point: it is God who initiates the relationship. God has first loved us, and our vocation is to respond to that love (cf. 1 Jn. 4:10). And not only does God initiate the relationship, He even goes looking for us, to the point of becoming one like us in the Incarnation. Pope John Paul II beautifully expresses this insight:

> Christianity has its starting-point in the Incarnation of the Word. Here, it is not simply a case of man seeking God, but of God who comes in Person to speak to man of himself and to show him the path by which he may be reached. . . . In *Jesus Christ* God not only speaks to man but also *seeks him out*. The Incarnation of the Son of God attests that God goes in search of man. . . . It is a search which *begins in the heart of God* and culminates in the Incarnation of the Word. If God goes in search of man, created in his own image and likeness, he does so because he loves him eternally in the Word, and wishes to raise him in Christ to the dignity of an adopted son.[3]

This awesome truth helps us to see the Eucharist in a new light. Before we enter God's world as His beloved children, He first enters ours. Since the preeminent way that God remains in our world is through the Holy Eucharist, then the Eucharist must give us important clues as to why Christ assumed human nature in the first place (cf. *Catechism*, nos. 456–60). The Eucharist points not so much to God's "inaccessible transcendence" as it does to the "divine condescension."[4]

---

[3] Pope John Paul II, Apostolic Letter on Preparation for the Jubilee Year 2000 *Tertio Millennio Adveniente* (November 10, 1994), nos. 6–7, emphasis in original.

[4] Pope John Paul II, Letter on the Mystery and Worship of the Eucharist *Dominicae Cenae* (February 24, 1980), no. 7.

Our heavenly Father has willed our existence from all eternity, has called each one of us by name, and has prepared a place for each one of us in heaven. While we remain free to reject His gift of salvation, He does desire "all men to be saved and to come to the knowledge of the truth" (1 Tim. 2:4).

As Our Lord teaches, what human father would give his son a stone when he asks for a loaf of bread? (cf. Mt. 7:9). In other words, even flawed human fathers strive to do right by their children. How much more has our heavenly Father taken into account our needs and desires in His plan of salvation for us, His wayward children. His will for us is truly "for our own good" or, as we profess more formally in the Creed, "for us men and for our salvation."

We can see this in our Lord's response to criticism of His disciples who were picking heads of grain on the Sabbath, "The sabbath was made for man, not man for the sabbath" (Mk. 2:27). In keeping the Lord's day (*dies Domini*), we are not submitting to oppressive, arbitrary rules. Nor should we be seeking merely to avoid violating the Third Commandment. Rather, the Lord's Day is for our good; our participation in Sunday Mass and observing a day of rest corresponds with the basic human need to worship God outwardly, publicly, and regularly (cf. Catechism, no. 2176), and our need to put our consuming human endeavors in their proper context.

Similarly, our Lord has taken the initiative with respect to the Eucharist. He gives it to us as a memorial of His suffering and death, and commands us to "do this" in His memory. He further advises us that if we fail to avail ourselves of the Eucharist, then we have no life in us (cf. Jn. 6:53). Our Lord assuredly does not place unnecessary stumbling blocks on the road to His Father's house. Rather, as a God who sought us out, who is intimately involved with the human family and who knows what's best for us, He gives us His own Body and Blood to help us experience the salvation He won for us, and to strengthen us in our Christian pilgrimage. It's incumbent upon us, then, to thank the Lord for this sublime gift and to beg Him to increase our faith and devotion. Then we can in some way relive the "Eucharistic amazement" of the disciples who, on the road to Emmaus, recognized Jesus in the breaking of the bread (cf. Lk. 24:30–31; *EE* 6).

"You Are the Light of the World" (Mt. 5:14)

The Church is the light to the nations. In fact, the central document of the Second Vatican Council, on the mystery of the Church, bears the Latin title *Lumen Gentium*, or "Light of the Nations."

Indeed, the mission of the Church is to shine the light of Christ to the world, to extend Christ through space and time. Christ's explicit instructions to His Church before ascending to His Father amounted to a sacred commissioning: His apostles were sent into the whole world so as to make disciples of all nations (cf. Mt. 28:18–20; Mk. 16:15). For this reason, it can rightly be said that the Church's perennial mission is evangelization.[5]

Pope John Paul II's 2003 encyclical letter on the Eucharist focuses on the intimate connection between the Eucharist and the Church, as the latter draws her

---

[5] Cf. Pope Paul VI, Apostolic Exhortation *Evangelii Nuntiandi* (December 8, 1975), nos. 13–14; Pope John Paul II, Encyclical on the Value and Inviolability of Human Life *Evangelium Vitae* (March 25, 1995), no. 78; see also chapter XI.

life from the former (*EE* 1). This speaks volumes as to the desired, life-giving effects of receiving our Lord in Holy Communion.

In this regard, the Holy Father draws an important parallel between the individual believer and the Blessed Virgin Mary at the Visitation (cf. Lk. 1:39–56). He writes that when the Blessed Mother "bore in her womb the Word made flesh, she became in some way a 'tabernacle'—the first 'tabernacle' in history—in which the Son of God, still invisible to our human gaze, allowed himself to be adored by Elizabeth, radiating his light as it were through the eyes and the voice of Mary" (*EE* 55).

When we receive Christ in us, just as our Lady received Him in her womb, it's not merely a private, "me and Jesus" matter. He does not desire to remain hidden within us. That would be like trying to put the light of Christ under a bushel basket (cf. Mt. 5:15). So, when Christ comes to us in Communion, it's not to diminish, impede, or conceal His light, but to multiply it! He uses each one of us as His lamps in the world. Lamps of themselves provide no light, but act as conduits of the light provided by an energy source. Similarly, we are not the "light of the world" except inasmuch as the Lord shines through us, as He did through she who was "full of grace" (Lk. 1:28). All generations call Mary blessed (cf. Lk. 1:48) precisely because of the singular way she "magnified" the light of Christ through her cooperation with divine grace.

The intensity of the light of Christ that we are able to bring to the world is dependent upon our own cooperation with divine grace. This again points to the need to be properly disposed to receive our Lord in Communion. The Church teaches that "[a]nyone conscious of a grave sin must receive the sacrament of Reconciliation before coming to communion" (*Catechism*, no. 1385). We further dispose ourselves by observing the required fast, as well as through the way we dress and conduct ourselves at Mass (cf. *Catechism*, no. 1387). In a spirit of praise, gratitude, and wonderment, we should recognize that Holy Communion is the moment when our Lord comes to us most intimately and completely. Similarly, after Communion, we should take ample time in prayer and thanksgiving, fostering an interior awareness of Christ in us lest we allow the "busy-ness" of our daily lives to obscure the light of Christ.

"For Behold, I Create New Heavens and a New Earth" (Is. 65:17)

In the Eucharist, heaven and earth actually meet. However, we are not instantly whisked away to a place where every tear is wiped away, where there is no more suffering and death (cf. Rev. 21:1–4). In a real sense, we have one foot in heaven while the other remains planted on this earth. This reality must affect every aspect of our lives during our sojourn here below. Pope John Paul II explains it this way: "Certainly the Christian vision leads to the expectation of 'new heavens' and 'a new earth' (Rev. 21:1), but this increases, rather than lessens, *our sense of responsibility for the world today*. I wish to reaffirm this forcefully at the beginning of the new millennium, so that Christians will feel more obliged than ever not to neglect their duties as citizens in this world" (*EE* 20).[6]

---

[6] See Fr. Frank Pavone's excellent article "Eucharistic Citizenship," found at www.priests forlife.org/columns/columns2003/03-07-28eucharisticcitizenship.htm.

It's significant that the Holy Father calls us "citizens *in* this world." As we await a new heavens and a new earth, we are called to be citizens in the world, but not of it (cf. Jn. 17:14–16). Vatican II's renewed emphasis on the role of the laity in the Church does not mean that we are to be removed from the world, which is the specific vocation of hermits, monks, and cloistered nuns. Rather, we function in the midst of the world as a leaven, as we participate in the renewal of all things in Christ (cf. Eph. 1:10).

Our participation in worldly endeavors must reflect the virtue of Christian hope. We're pilgrims, which implies that we are on a journey, and not simply waiting at a bus stop. Therefore, what we do now matters. Yet, "pilgrimage" also implies that we are away from home, so at the same time we must continually look beyond the limitations of this world—in other words, we should not get too comfortable here. Vatican II expresses the necessary balance this way:

> [T]he expectation of a new earth must not weaken but rather stimulate our concern for cultivating this one. For here grows the body of a new human family, a body which even now is able to give some kind of foreshadowing of the new age.
>
> Hence, while earthly progress must be carefully distinguished from the growth of Christ's kingdom, to the extent that the former can contribute to the better ordering of human society, it is of vital concern to the Kingdom of God.
>
> . . . On this earth that kingdom is already present in mystery. When the Lord returns it will be brought into full flower. (*GS* 39)

Authentic Christian living, then, entails working to foster peace and solidarity among nations. It means that we should be tireless in protecting the most vulnerable in our midst, especially the unborn, oppressed, elderly, and dying. It means that the light of Christ should shine through us and help order all human endeavors and institutions in accordance with the Gospel, realizing that our feeble efforts will not reach their perfection in this life.

Here I should emphasize two necessary components of Christian discipleship. First, authentic Christian living necessarily entails our own commitment to moral rectitude. As we repeatedly hear in Scripture, if we love the Lord, we will keep His commandments (cf. Jn. 15:10). Second, mercy must characterize our Christian discipleship. We continually need divine mercy ourselves, and we also must be instruments or ambassadors of divine mercy to others (cf. 2 Cor. 5:18–20). Christian living is an intensely personal matter. We don't simply care for the poor or the sick or the lame in the abstract, but rather, our Eucharistic Lord communicates His love through us in our personal encounters with others. For this reason, the Church encourages all the faithful to perform corporal and spiritual works of mercy.[7]

Lay people not only participate in the world, but also, in an analogous way, in the Church and in the celebration of Mass. There is once again an important balance that must be kept in tension. Lay people

---

[7] The corporal works of mercy, drawn from Matthew 25:34–36 are feeding the hungry, giving drink to the thirsty, welcoming strangers, clothing the naked, visiting the sick, and visiting those in prison. The spiritual works of mercy are instructing the ignorant, converting sinners, advising the perplexed, comforting the sorrowful, showing patience to sinners and those who err, forgiving others, and praying for the living and the dead (cf. *Catechism*, no. 2447).

are neither called to a clericalism that would "leave everything to Father," nor is their participation in the Church in conflict with the role of the clergy, such that lay people should feel compelled to usurp the priest's distinctive role.

We see this in a particular way at Mass. On the one hand, the ordained priest is absolutely indispensable to a valid celebration of the Mass. Only the sacrament of Holy Orders confers the power to act in the person of Christ and thereby consecrate the Eucharist (*Catechism*, no. 1548). If there's no priest, there's no Mass. Pope John Paul II bluntly affirms that the Eucharist is "*a gift which radically transcends the power of the assembly* and is in any event essential for validly linking the Eucharistic consecration to the sacrifice of the Cross and to the Last Supper" (*EE* 29, emphasis in original).

Yet at the same time, the laity's participation is not irrelevant, as though the Mass were something that should just go on without us. Cardinal Newman once pointed out that the priest would look rather silly up there without a congregation. But even more, each person is called to an active participation through the exercise of the priesthood of the laity—a priesthood in which all baptized Christians participate (cf. 1 Pet. 2:9; *SC* 14). All of us are called to unite our own unique prayers, activities, joys, concerns, and sufferings to Christ's sacrifice. That is the "fully conscious and active participation" at Mass envisioned by Vatican II (*SC* 14). That is the authentic priesthood of the laity, which differs "in essence and not only in degree" from the ordained priesthood (*LG* 10). And that is the foundation for our participation as disciples in the world, but not of it, as we await the world that is to come.

"You, therefore, Must Be Perfect, as Your Heavenly Father Is Perfect" (Mt. 5:48)

We believe that through transubstantiation bread and wine cease to be bread and wine but truly become the Body and Blood of Jesus Christ, even though all the physical properties, such as size, taste, appearance, and composition, remain the same. We cannot see the difference, but we accept this teaching through the vision of faith.

But the sacraments effect an analogous change in each one of us. A baby girl right after she is baptized looks exactly the same as she did before, yet she is a child of God and a member of Christ's body, the Church (see *Catechism*, nos. 1262–74). A young man, once he wipes off all the holy oil, looks the same right after his Ordination, but now he is able to consecrate the Eucharist and to forgive sins in God's name. And we sinners look the same after we walk out of the confessional, but we have had our relationship with the Lord restored and renewed. In all cases, we look the same on the outside, but at the core of our being we've been radically changed.

It's no different with the Eucharist. As Pope St. Leo the Great wrote in the fifth century, "the partaking of the Body and Blood of Christ has no less an effect than to change us into what we have received."[8] The eternal Word of God took on flesh so that we might participate in the divine life, that we might truly become what we eat. The transformation of a sinner into a saint is the goal of every Christian life without exception. Therefore, all of us must be committed to leading changed, "Eucharistic" lives (cf. *EE* 20).

---

[8] Saint Leo the Great, *Sermones*, 63, no. 7; *Patrologia Latina* 54, 357C.

We use the Latin expression *ex opere operato* (literally, from the work having been done) to express the guarantee that Christ's Real Presence and superabundant grace will be available at every validly celebrated Mass. However, just as we benefit from food's nutrients only if we digest the food well, we benefit from the grace of the Eucharist only to the extent we effectively digest this spiritual food.

The Pope likens our "Amen" when we receive Communion to our Lady's fiat at the Annunciation, when she consents to our Lord's making His dwelling in her virginal womb (cf. Lk. 1:26–38; *EE* 55). Our Amen, in a real way, gives the Lord permission to come in, change us imperceptibly from within, and orient us toward our true and eternal good. But this "Amen," this permission, often comes with strings attached on our part, as we don't necessarily want Him to change *everything*. Nevertheless, He gently and relentlessly teaches us through the Eucharist that we will find our ultimate happiness in giving ourselves away to God and neighbor without reserve.

The Christian life is characterized by the interior balance of the contemplative Mary and the active Martha, both of whom are honored as saints. Indeed, at the beginning of the new millennium, all of us Marthas are called to roll up ours sleeves and actively participate in the great work of the new evangelization.

Even so, Scripture is very clear. Our Lord said that Mary chose the better part (cf. Lk. 10:42). For us, Our Lord is present at every Mass and in every tabernacle throughout the world. If we truly want to live authentic Christian lives, we do well to return, frequently and with much love and devotion, to the Source: Jesus, our Eucharistic Lord.

Leon J. Suprenant, Jr. is the president of Catholics United for the Faith. He received his law degree from the University of Missouri-Kansas City School of Law and his master's degree in theology from Franciscan University of Steubenville. He is coeditor of Catholic for a Reason, *vol. 1 and* FAITH FACTS, *vols. 1 and 2, and editor of* Catholic for a Reason II, *and* Servants of the Gospel *(Emmaus Road). He is a frequent contributor to* National Catholic Register *and other Catholic periodicals.*

CHAPTER X

The Mass and Evangelization

CURTIS MARTIN

You Wait Here

If you have ever brought a non-Catholic friend to Mass, you have probably felt the tension. They become a bit uncomfortable as they enter the church; everyone around them is dipping their fingers into water and then wiping it off on their heads and chests. As they sit down, people around them are falling to their knees, as if they were Roman soldiers in the presence of the Emperor. When the priest comes in, he speaks to the congregation, and everyone, except your friend, seems to know the right responses. Then when it is time for Communion you have to say, "Wait here, I'll be right back." What you had hoped would be an occasion to share your faith with a friend seems to be an awkward moment that only alienates him.

Is the Church saying "no" to non-Catholics? Not exactly. What the Church really says is, "Wait."

Imagine that you have a daughter who, after grad-
uating from college meets a great young man, who is
virtuous, faithful, and loves her very much. She brings
him home to meet you, and he asks your permission
to marry her. You find yourself wanting to welcome
him into your family. This is how the Church feels
about non-Catholics. She is eager to welcome them
into her fold. But first things first; before there is
going to be real intimacy, there needs to be a wedding.

In marriage, the physical intimacy, which would
be sinful before the wedding, becomes sacred afterwards. The sacrament of Holy Matrimony is the
door though which the spouses must pass through
before they become one. So too, for non-Catholics
who want to receive the Eucharist, the physical intimacy of receiving Jesus Christ bodily is designed for
a lifelong covenantal relationship with Jesus in His
Church. Everyone is welcome, but first things first.

The Mass is the wedding feast of the Lamb, and
if we are to attend, we are to do so as the Bride.[1]
"The entire Christian life bears the mark of the spousal love of Christ and the Church. Already Baptism,
the entry into the People of God, is a nuptial mystery,
it is so to speak the nuptial bath [cf. Eph. 5:26–27]
which precedes the wedding feast, the Eucharist"
(*Catechism*, no. 1617).

The Book of Revelation presents Jesus Christ
meeting His Bride, the Church, for a wedding feast
that precedes the unveiling. This is profoundly intimate language. Spousal love is a God given icon of
the relationship Christ desires with us, a relationship
that reaches full communion in the Mass.

---

[1] For norms regarding Communion, see *Code of Canon Law*
(Washington, DC: Canon Law Society of America, 1983), can. 844.

Mass is the consummation of a love story, and to understand it, we must go back to the beginning. This love story begins through evangelization. In evangelization, our goal is not simply to get people to go to Church, or even simply to get them to go to Heaven. The goal is to allow Jesus to reach their hearts—to woo them into full earthly Communion.

When I asked my wife Michaelann on our first date, I asked her to go to dinner with me. Did I want her simply to go to dinner with me? No! I wanted her to *want* to go to dinner with me. If she had accepted merely because she was hungry, I would have failed. As our desire for one another blossomed into romance, we found ourselves wanting to be together more and more. Eventually, our shared desire led us to come before God and pledge our lifelong love in the sacrament of Marriage.

So how do we as Catholics share our faith and draw others into relationship with Jesus? What would you say to someone who wanted to know why you were Catholic? If you are like many Catholics you might begin with, "Umm. . . . Well, I was raised Catholic. . . . " This is a good reason for being Catholic, but it does not really answer the question. Being raised Catholic is a great way to become a Catholic, but what about those who were not? The real question, behind the one asked, is, "Is there any reason why I should consider becoming Catholic?"

We should be ready to explain our faith at all times; Saint Peter put it this way, "[B]ut in your hearts reverence Christ as Lord. Always be prepared to make a defense to any one who calls you to account for the hope that is in you, yet do it with gentleness and reverence" (1 Pet. 3:15). Our willingness and

ability to share our faith should overflow naturally
from the joy in our lives. As we share our faith, the
Mass plays an irreplaceable role, but in a way you
might not at first think.

The Mass and Evangelization

Evangelicals invite people to their church services to evangelize them. Using the Mass the way
Evangelicals use their church services can be awkward. Just as the Holy Eucharist is more than a mere
piece of bread that only symbolizes Jesus, the Mass
is more than a mere church service. Because of the
radical difference between the Mass and other church
services, we can't do what Evangelicals can—we can
do much more.

Imagine a man who goes down to the local dealer-
ship to buy a Sport Utility Vehicle (SUV). He selects
the one he wants, haggles over the price, and buys it.
He walks out to the lot, opens the door, throws the
keys on the seat and begins to push his new car home.
After a very short distance, he begins to regret his
purchase. Maybe he should have purchased a smaller
car; this one is so hard to push. As he passes other
cars parked on the side of the road, he sees one car
after another that would be easier to push than his
SUV, and his regret turns to frustration.

We all see his problem; the man is frustrated
because he is not using his SUV in the way it is intended. If he got into his SUV, he would see that it was not
a great burden; rather it would be able to carry great
burdens for him. So it is with the Mass and evangelization. We need to see the Mass for the gift it is,
given to us by Jesus Christ. When we *use* it properly,
it prepares, inspires, and completes our efforts.

The role of Mass in evangelization is explained in the Second Vatican Council. "The Eucharist is 'the *source* and *summit* of the Christian life' [*LG* 11] 'The other sacraments, and indeed all ecclesiastical ministries and works of apostolate, are bound up with the Eucharist and are oriented toward it' [*PO* 5]" (*Catechism*, no. 1324, emphasis added).

The Eucharist is the *source* of our evangelistic efforts; it is from our communion with Jesus Christ that all of our efforts must flow. The Eucharist is also the *summit* of our evangelistic efforts; it is towards full communion that our evangelistic efforts should flow. But, in between, we are to take the reality of the Mass into our own lives and make Christ present in the world through our actions and words. As the *Catechism* explains, "'The sacred liturgy does not exhaust the entire activity of the Church' [*SC* 9]: it must be preceded by evangelization, faith and conversion. It can then produce its fruits in the lives of the faithful; new life in the Spirit, involvement in the mission of the Church, and service to her unity" (*Catechism*, no. 1072).

More Than Meets the Eye

When we come to Mass, we enter into worship of God. I say "enter into" because the worship exists whether we are there or not. In the heavenly Jerusalem, the Blessed Trinity is worshipped day and night. The Mass is a real, but veiled participation in the heavenly worship. This is how the Church describes the Mass: "[B]y the Eucharistic celebration we already unite ourselves with the heavenly liturgy and anticipate eternal life" (*Catechism*, no. 1326). "In the earthly liturgy we take part in a foretaste of that heavenly liturgy which is celebrated in the holy city of Jerusalem" (*SC* 8).

In the Mass, we are united with all the saints and holy angels, including your particular guardian angel and the guardian angels of every person we will ever meet. Think of what Jesus Himself said about the guardian angels, "See that you do not despise one of these little ones; for I tell you that in heaven their angels always behold the face of my Father who is in heaven" (Mt. 18:10). Each person has a guardian angel with the primary responsibility of guiding that person through life. The Mass is the perfect time to ask the Holy Spirit for help in the work of evangelization, to ask your guardian angel to help you be aware of opportunities that arise, and to beseech the guardian angels of everyone you will meet to entreat God for the grace of forgiveness and conversion. It is this sense of mission that gives the Eucharistic liturgy its title, "*Holy Mass* (*Missa*), because the liturgy in which the mystery of salvation is accomplished concludes with a sending forth (*missio*) of the faithful, so that they may fulfill God's will in their daily lives" (*Catechism*, no. 1332).

Full participation in the Mass is for those who are already fully incorporated into the Church. In fact, in the early Church, catechumens, those who had converted to Christ but had not yet been fully initiated through Baptism, would attend Mass, listen to the readings from Sacred Scripture and the teaching of the priest. Then they would be excused before the second part of the Mass, the liturgy of the Eucharist, began. The Eucharist was reserved for the fully initiated Christians.

Once baptized, the new Christians would receive Jesus in the Eucharist as the consummation of evangelization. "'The liturgy is the summit towards which the activity of the Church is directed; it is also the font from which all her power flows' [SC 10] It is therefore the privileged place for catechizing the People of God. 'Catechesis is intrinsically linked with the whole of liturgical and sacramental activity, for it is in the sacraments especially in the Eucharist that Christ Jesus works in fullness for the transformation of men' [John Paul II, CT 23]" (*Catechism*, no. 1074).

Seen in this light, evangelization is to the Mass, what courtship is to marriage. As a young couple gets to know one another more and more, their hearts long to be together. As they prepare for marriage, they learn what marriage entails. Only then is it time for marriage—a lifelong, covenantal commitment, and conjugal union. So too, evangelization is designed to awaken a love for God, and gratitude for His forgiveness and for all of His gifts. As an individual prepares for Holy Communion, this new convert should learn what the Christian life entails. Only then can the convert receive Baptism—a lifelong commitment, and the intimacy of Eucharistic Communion.

The Great Commission

The last words of Jesus on earth were, "All authority in heaven and earth has been given to me. Go therefore and make disciples of all the nations, baptizing them in the name of the Father and of the Son and of the Holy Spirit, teaching them to observe all that I have commanded you; and lo, I am with you always, to the close of the age" (Mt. 28:18–20).

The "Great Commission," has several distinctive points. First, Jesus Christ has been given all authority. He then sends His disciples out to make disciples of the nations. He says, "Go therefore . . ."—and whenever you see the word "therefore" in Scripture, you should check to see what it is there for. In this case, the authority of Christ is precisely the reason we need to go make disciples of the nations, and He will be with us.

Jesus gives us two gifts to fulfill the Great Commission. First, He gives the fullness of His teaching—we are to teach *all* that He commanded. Second, He gives us Himself—we are to share the Real Presence of Jesus. The Catholic Church is the one place where we find both of these gifts.

The goal of evangelization is to introduce someone to Jesus Christ and to the Church He founded. We share how Jesus continues His saving presence on earth through His Mystical Body, the Church. As Christ Himself said to His disciples, "He who hears you hears me, and he who rejects you rejects me, and he who rejects me rejects him who sent me" (Lk. 10:16). Jesus is the vine and the members of His Church are the branches. In light of Jesus' teaching, to speak of loving Christ without loving His Church makes no sense at all.

Catholic faith is a faith in who Jesus is, and in all that He has done through His life, teaching, death, and Resurrection, and through the Catholic Church. Catholic faith is both described and implored when we pray the *Act of Faith*:

> O my God, I firmly believe that You are one God in three Divine Persons, Father, Son and Holy Ghost; I believe that Your divine Son became man,

and died for our sins, and that He will come to judge the living and the dead. I believe these and all the truths which the Holy Catholic Church teaches, because You have revealed them, who can neither deceive nor be deceived.

Commitment to Christ through His Church is the commitment that evangelization seeks so that someone can begin to receive the Holy Eucharist worthily.

Reasons Why Catholics Don't Evangelize

So, why don't Catholics evangelize?

Many Catholics are not comfortable as evangelists. In our modern world, we are trained to live and let live, not to *impose* our views upon others. But, as we have seen, these attitudes have to be reexamined in light of Jesus' Great Commission. We ought not to impose our views on others, but we have been commissioned by Christ Himself to charitably *propose* the truth of the Catholic faith to everyone. If we take a deeper look, we can see at least six reasons why many Catholics are hesitant to share their faith with others:

Lack of belief in objective truth.[2] As long as religion is seen only as a matter of preference, then our missionary zeal is thwarted. Catholics don't believe that Jesus is God only for Christians; we must believe that He is God, period. If Jesus is God, then those who do not accept His claims of divinity are wrong—not evil—but wrong, broken by sin and in need of the healing and forgiveness that only Jesus can give. Telling someone about the forgiveness of Jesus Christ

---

[2] For further reflection on this point, see *Catechism*, nos. 172, 174,181, 843, 849, 851.

should be like telling someone suffering from cancer about a cure.

A misunderstanding of the Church.[3] Many people view separation from God as the only problem caused by sin. This is certainly the most significant effect, but not the only one. God originally created us to share kinship with Him and with one another. Humanity is intended to be a family. Salvation history can be summarized as God's gracious initiative to reconstitute the broken family of Adam into the family of God. Being disinherited from God's family through sin is precisely what we are saved from.

A reluctance to use the name of "Jesus."[4] Evangelization is essentially making an introduction, and in order to introduce someone, you must know his name. Catholics seem to be comfortable speaking about "the Lord," but find it more difficult to use the name, "Jesus." Ironically and tragically, the name of our Lord is sometimes only heard when used in vain. Others, who would never dream of offending our Lord, show a sort of misguided reverence by never speaking His holy name. Listen to wisdom of Mother Church: "But the one name that contains everything is the one that the Son of God received in his incarnation: Jesus. The divine name may not be spoken by human lips, but by assuming our humanity The Word of God hands it over to us and we can invoke it: 'Jesus,' 'YHWH saves' [cf. Ex. 3:14; 33:19–23; Mt. 1:21]" (*Catechism*, no. 2666).

---

[3] See *Catechism*, nos. 845–852, 959. For a compelling explanation of the Church, see Henri De Lubac, *The Splendor of the Church* (San Francisco: Ignatius Press, 1986).
[4] For further reflection see *Catechism*, no. 2145.

If you don't live it, you can't give it.[5] Witness is absolutely essential. As Saint Francis of Assisi stated, "Preach the Gospel at all times, if necessary use words." Our words mean little if they don't flow from a transformed life. You cannot give that which you do not have.

We may not love Christ, the Church, or others enough. "Our love for Jesus and for our neighbor impels us to speak to others about our faith" (Catechism, no. 166). We believe that Jesus is truly God, "And there is salvation in no one else, for there is no other name under heaven that has been given among men, by which they may be saved" (Acts 4:12). We see the Church, not as a mere human institution, but as the very Family of God, the Mystical Body of Christ, the Bride of Christ and our Mother, as Saint Cyprian said, "He can no longer have God for his Father, who has not the Church for his Mother."[6] Therefore, how can we withhold this good news from others, if we truly love them?

We don't know what to say. The remainder of this chapter is designed to give you some suggestions of how to lead someone to Christ.

---

[5] For further reflection see *Catechism*, no. 852–854.

[6] *On the Unity of the Church*, no. 6 in *Ante-Nicene Fathers*, vol. 5, eds. Alexander Roberts and James Donaldson (Peabody, MA: Hendrickson, 1994), 423.

See also, Pope Paul VI, Apostolic Exhortation *Evangelii Nuntiandi* (December 8, 1975), no. 16: "[N]ot without sorrow we can hear people—whom we wish to believe are well-intentioned but who are certainly misguided in their attitude—continually claiming to love Christ but without the Church."

Relational Evangelization

All true evangelization is motivated by love: love of God and love of our neighbor. Both the message and the model of our efforts must be Jesus Christ. He spoke to the masses, but Jesus' style was also deeply interpersonal as he spent significant time with a few. He invested His life in them and asked them to do the same. Saint Paul shares this principle with the early church: "So, being affectionately desirous of you, we were ready to share with you not only the gospel of God but also our own selves, because you had become very dear to us" (1 Thess. 2:8).

By investing our lives in people, we develop relationships, and within those relationships, we will have opportunities to share our faith. Evangelists are most successful when they have earned the right to be heard. Friendship is an end in itself; we are called to love people, period. But, if we love them, we will share what is most important in our life. If we have seen a great movie or read a great book, we will find opportunities to share this with our friends—how much more if we have discovered new life in Jesus?

There are at least three ways to begin a spiritual conversation:

Direct Method:
"How important is God in your life?"
"Do you believe in God?"
"Have you ever thought about becoming Catholic?"

Indirect Method:
FRIEND: "What did you do this weekend?"
    Instead of responding "Not much, just relaxed."

YOU: "I went to an awesome conference in Denver with some great people I've met. I learned about Christ centered principles for leadership."

If your friend is interested, he will ask questions about the conference, providing you an opportunity to share your faith. If not, he will simply change the subject.

Invitational Method:
"Next week Dr. Edward Sri is speaking about Christlike leadership at the University. I'm going, would you like to come? I can give you a ride."

Principles for Starting a Spiritual Conversation

Before we begin our conversations, we need to be prepared. Here are some helpful steps that prepare us to share the Gospel.

—*Pray* for opportunities, and for the grace to recognize them.
—Take genuine *interest* in people, and share your love for Jesus with them.
—Be courageous in *taking risks*—this is the key.
—Take *every opportunity*, even split second ones.
—Always have an attitude of *love*—our motivation should be the same as God's.
—Leave the *results* to God.

Talking about the Faith

First, we need a useful definition of successful evangelization: It is offering a meaningful introduction to Jesus Christ and life within His Church, and then leaving the results to the Holy Spirit. How do

we share the Gospel message? Here are some basic
and essential points that we should cover.[7]

A Loving Father. God is our Father; He created us
in His image and likeness to be His children. His
desire is to share His life and love—both here and
in heaven. God is love. Many people today do not
understand this and view God as a tyrant who wants
to dominate and subjugate us. We can share God's
intent as revealed in Scripture: "I have loved you with
an everlasting love; therefore I have continued my
faithfulness to you" (Jer. 31:3).

Sin Breaks a Relationship. Through sin, we turn away
from God and reject His fatherly love. This rebellion
has broken our fellowship with Him, resulting in
alienation from God and one another. Sin has also
destroyed the family God created. Sin has resulted in
spiritual death. We are unable to repair this condition
through our own efforts and we are in desperate need
of help. As Scripture says: "[A]ll have sinned and fall-
en short of the glory of God" (Rom. 3:23).

Restoration in Christ. By His life, death and
Resurrection Jesus restores us to a relationship with
God. Through Jesus Christ, God's only Son, we can
receive forgiveness of sins and adoption as sons and
daughters of God, and can be welcomed back into
fellowship with God and with one another. Jesus is
the Savior of the world. "For as by one man's dis-

---

[7] The following is adapted from Real Life © 2003- FOCUS, a Gospel
presentation used with permission by Fellowship of Catholic University
Students. You can obtain copies of this presentation, as well as other
tools to help explain these basic aspects of the Christian life, at www.
focusonline.org. Ask for their "Evangelization Follow-ups."

obedience many were made sinners, so by one man's obedience many will be made righteous" (Rom. 5:19).

Reborn in Baptism. Jesus offers His forgiveness freely, but we need to respond. Through Baptism, we are reborn with the very life of God in our souls, and we are welcomed back into the family of God, the Church.

It is not enough to know that Jesus died and rose from the dead; we need to repent and be baptized. We must respond to God's grace, give up our self-centered life, and allow Jesus Christ to become the Lord of our life. Through Baptism, the Holy Spirit is given to us, making it possible for us to begin living the Christian life. The first step is simply to ask God for forgiveness and commit to come home to Him and to His family, the Church. "Repent and be baptized every one of you in the name of Jesus Christ for the forgiveness of your sins; and you shall receive the gift of the Holy Spirit" (Acts 2:38).

Members of God's Family. Jesus saves us into God's family. Through faith and the sacraments, Jesus gives us the Holy Spirit, making us sons and daughters of God. We are not merely saved *from* sin, but saved *into* God's family, the Church. Jesus gives us His Father as our Father, His Mother as our Mother, and His brothers and sisters become ours as well. The Church is God's plan of salvation.

We must see that salvation has consequences. Because of sin, we were alienated from God's fatherly love and from one another. God's solution is to reconstitute the fallen family of humanity into the redeemed family of God, the Church. "[F]or in Christ Jesus you are all sons of God, through faith. For as many of you were baptized into Christ have put on Christ. There is neither Jew nor Greek, there is neither slave nor free, there is neither male nor female; for you are all one in Christ Jesus" (Gal. 3:26–28).

A Moment and a Life Style

Pentecost provides a model for us in our evangelization. After days of prayer in the same room where Jesus offered the first Mass, the Apostles and Mary, the Mother Jesus, are filled with the Holy Spirit. Peter, together with the other apostles, proclaims the Gospel to the crowds. When Peter finishes, the people cry out, "What shall we do?" Peter responds, that they must repent and be baptized for the forgiveness of their sins (cf. Acts 2:38).

Repentance and Baptism are not the end; they are the beginning of the Christian life. Just a few verses later, we see how the new Christians spent their time. "And they devoted themselves to the apostles' teaching, and fellowship, to the breaking of bread and the prayers" (Act 2:42). This model of Christian life is, not coincidentally, exactly what the Catholic Church still teaches today. In 1992, the Catholic Church published its most recent universal catechism. Its four-fold structure is exactly the same as the previous universal catechism published in 1566. Notice that it follows the biblical pattern:

Part One: "The apostles' teaching," specifically the Apostles' Creed;

Part Two: "The breaking of the bread," and the other sacraments, where Christ's saving work is communicated to individual Christians;

Part Three: "Fellowship," or how we live out the two great commandments of love of God and neighbor;

Part Four: "Prayer"—God has made us for Himself; the ultimate reason for our creation and our redemption is that we might live in communion with our heavenly Father.

How do we begin to follow the scriptural pattern of evangelization? First, we attend Mass with great love and renewed vision, knowing that Jesus, in the Eucharist, is the source of our life and of our evangelization. Then, we build authentic friendships where we can share what matters most to us—Jesus and the Christian life. Finally, as God leads our beloved brothers and sisters to conversion, we can continue to share the faith with them and prepare them for full covenantal communion with Jesus in the Church. Then they too can faithfully receive the Body, Blood, Soul and Divinity of Jesus Christ in Holy Communion and begin their role in the Great Commission (cf. Mt. 28:18–20).

John Paul II echoes Christ's words, "The Church's mission stands in continuity with the mission of Christ: 'As the Father has sent me, even so I send you' (Jn. 20:21). From the perpetuation of the sacrifice of the Cross and her communion with the body and blood of Christ in the Eucharist, the Church draws the spiritual power needed to carry out her mission. The Eucharist thus appears as both *the source* and *the summit* of all evangelization, since its goal is the communion of mankind with Christ and in him with the Father and the Holy Spirit" (*EE* 22, emphasis in original).

Curtis Martin is the founding president of the Fellowship of Catholic University Students (FOCUS), a dynamic evangelization and leadership training program for college students, http://www.focusonline.org. Curtis is coauthor of Boys to Men: The Transforming Power of Virtue *(Emmaus Road) and* Family Matters: A Bible Study on Marriage and Family *(Emmaus Road), which he wrote with his wife, Michaelann, who is the author of* Woman of Grace: A Bible Study for Married Women *(Emmaus Road).*

CHAPTER XI

Suffering and the Mass
The Great Exchange

JEFF CAVINS

Pope John Paul II said, "Down through the centuries and generations it has been seen that in suffering there is concealed a particular power that draws a person interiorly close to Christ, a special grace."[1]

How many times have you heard someone say, "The Mass is boring," or "What does the Mass have to do with my situation in life?" How many of us have grown up not understanding that in the Mass we have the divine drama of sacrificial love presented to us with the invitation to participate in the ultimate act of love? Unfortunately, for some, the Mass becomes a duty of time where images, scents, responses, and movements swirl about to make up what we call religion.

The most ironic thing about many people's experience during Mass is that they have brought their

---

[1] Apostolic Letter on the Christian Meaning of Human Suffering *Salvifici Doloris* (February 11, 1984), no. 26, emphasis omitted.

problems, their suffering, and their preoccupations to the very place where their suffering can find true meaning. Why is it that we oftentimes review our life's difficulties in our minds, completely missing the very drama that changes the question mark in our hearts to an exclamation mark? Like the dehydrated man circling a drinking fountain contemplating how thirsty he is, so today, many Catholics are circling the Mass with thoughts of their own predicament.

In this chapter, we will focus on one aspect of the liturgy—suffering, and how Christ's suffering can transform our lives in the Mass. Every time we go to Mass, we should be struck by the fact that God has come to earth, suffered, died, and now asks us to follow in His footsteps. At the end of every Mass, we must leave with the attitude: Not only am I going to join myself to Him in His sacrifice, but I'm also going to live that sacrifice when I exit the door and go to my home, my work, and my neighbors. In short, I'm going to become like Jesus in every area of my life.

Often our lives are spent trying to avoid suffering. We don't like to suffer, and most of us have unanswered questions about suffering. Especially, we wonder how God, if He loves us, could allow us to suffer. The gospel message provides answers to the question of suffering, but those answers may not be readily apparent. Throughout salvation history, we see that the ways of God are often not the ways of man. Embedded in the dark confines of an oyster, we find, to our surprise, shining pearls. Perhaps the circumstances in which you find yourself appear to be dark and hopeless. But know: you are not alone. Not only have others been where you are, but more importantly, Jesus has been where you are.

SUFFERING AND THE MASS 185

Part of the problem of understanding the subject of suffering is that we are accustomed to quick answers, and we usually don't contemplate suffering until we are in the midst of it. When we are in the midst of suffering we usually are not focused or disciplined enough to wrestle with the biblical text, the writings of the Church Fathers, or the Tradition of the Church. Often we become stuck in the quicksand of our pain, distracted by difficulty, and feel that answers are just out of our reach. Furthermore, the pace of modern life dictates to us that we should be able to go to Mass, pray a quick prayer, and expect relief from our problems by the time we get back home for the football game.

The time to study the topic of suffering is before major problems of life occur. However, an academic study of suffering can only go so far. Suffering is part of the Christian vocation and can only be truly understood in the school of suffering. I became interested in suffering when, not too long ago, I found out that I had a split disk in my neck that caused excruciating pain. While I knew the teachings of the Church on redemptive suffering, I did not know how to put those teachings into practice in my life. I didn't understand why or how suffering could become a profitable ordeal.

There are various kinds of suffering. Physical suffering, such as a broken leg, neck pain, or cancer, can be quite intense and, if prolonged, can wear a person down. Spiritual, moral and emotional suffering, such as betrayal, depression, loss of a loved one, and disappointment, can often be worse than physical pain. Any kind of suffering can be devastating.

As we survey human history, it becomes evident

that it's not "if" we are going to suffer during our
lives, but "when," and, more importantly, "how" will
we suffer—poorly or well? Once the Holy Sacrifice
of the Mass is understood, it will become the key to
suffering well, rather than loosing hope in life. There
is meaning in suffering that can change your sorrow
into joy. I know—I've been there and have, like many
others, been transformed as a result of understanding
the message of the Mass.

When there is no meaning attached to suffering,
people can easily fall into despair. However, once
meaning is attached to suffering, it is astounding what
people can endure. The key is not the suffering, but
the meaning attached to it. Most would agree that
they would not be willing to endure great agony for
six months for a mouse, because they don't see any
meaning in their suffering for a mouse. But most
would enthusiastically raise their hands in affirmation
if I were to ask, "How many of you would be willing
to endure pain for your daughter or your son?" They
would raise their hands because they would find
meaning, namely the life of their child.

The key to understanding suffering is found in the
life, death, and Resurrection of Jesus Christ. When
asked, "Why did Jesus come to earth?" the answer
is usually, "He came to die for my sins." While this
is true, there must be more—for if He only came to
die then why wouldn't He have accepted death as an
infant? He was fully God as an infant, so why not
offer Himself shortly after being born? As we will see,
the mission of Jesus involves more than simply dying.
It involves a complete identification with humanity,
including suffering. We will also see that our mission
in life constitutes more than merely going to church

every week. We are called to not only attend Mass, but to completely identify with Christ by joining our lives to His.

At every Mass across the world, you will most likely see a crucifix made out of wood, metal, or some other material. It may be a simple cross or an expensive ornate one. The question is: Why did Jesus have to die such a death, and what does His death mean to you in your current problem?

In Luke 24, Jesus is walking with two men on the road to Emmaus shortly after His Resurrection. The gentlemen were sad, disappointed—in a word, they were suffering. They had thought that Jesus would restore the kingdom of God and redeem Israel. Though they did not recognize Jesus at this point on their journey, they were walking with God, talking to God, complaining about God. How ironic that these two men, in the midst of their suffering, did not know that the One who suffered for them was walking right beside them. Jesus finally says, "'O foolish men, and slow of heart to believe all that the prophets have spoken! Was it not necessary that the Christ should suffer these things and enter into his glory?' Then beginning with Moses and the prophets, Jesus interpreted to them in all the scriptures the things concerning himself" (vv. 25–27).

The question of our suffering begins with a more basic question: Why did God suffer? To answer this we must see the relationship between Adam and Jesus in terms of their relationship to God, the Father. The Apostle Paul sees a direct correlation between the fall of Adam and the victory of Christ. In 1 Corinthians 15:22, 45, he writes, "For as in Adam all die, so also in Christ shall all be made alive. . . . Thus it is written,

'The first man Adam became a living being'; the last Adam became a life-giving spirit."

Shortly after Adam and Eve's creation they underwent an ordeal in the Garden of Eden. Created in the image and likeness of God, Adam and Eve had an intellect and a will. In other words, they could know a thing and act on it. In the garden, Adam and Eve were given directives and a choice. Successful completion of this ordeal would give them the opportunity to fully enter into the life of the Trinity through obedience and sacrifice.

> And the LORD God planted a garden in Eden, in the east; and there he put the man whom he had formed. And out of the ground the LORD God made to grow every tree that is pleasant to the sight and good for food, the tree of life also in the midst of the garden, and the tree of the knowledge of good and evil. . . . The LORD God took the man and put him in the Garden of Eden to till it and keep it. And the LORD God commanded the man, saying, "You may freely eat of every tree of the garden; but of the tree of the knowledge of good and evil you shall not eat, for in the day that you eat of it you shall die." (Gen. 2:8–9, 15–17)

Adam was given two commands by God: Till and keep the garden and do not eat of the tree of the knowledge of good and evil. If Adam ate from the tree of the knowledge of good and evil, the consequences would be death. While Adam was immortal, his body "was mortal by nature, with a healthy, instinctive abhorrence of physical death."[2] The punishment of death had meaning to Adam because he understood the gravity of death. Shortly after God gave the two

2 Scott Hahn, *First Comes Love: Finding Your Family in the Church and the Trinity* (New York: Doubleday, 2002), 66.

commandments to Adam, Eve was fashioned from Adam, creating a spousal relationship. It's implied in the biblical text that Adam, as husband, would communicate God's commands to Eve.

In the Hebrew, we find an interesting word, "keep," that loses some of its impact in English translations. The Hebrew word for "keep" is *shamar* and means, "to guard." Adam was told to guard the garden and cultivate it. The command of God begs the question, guard against what? We don't know at this point in the text, but as we turn to the third chapter of Genesis it becomes clear.

> Now the serpent was more subtle than any other wild creature that the LORD God had made. He said to the woman, "Did God say, 'You shall not eat of any tree of the garden'?" And the woman said to the serpent, "We may eat of the fruit of the trees of the garden; but God said, 'You shall not eat of the fruit of the tree which is in the midst of the garden, neither shall you touch it, lest you die.'" But the serpent said to the woman, "You will not die. For God knows that when you eat of it your eyes will be opened, and you will be like God, knowing good and evil." So when the woman saw that the tree was good for food, and that it was a delight to the eyes, and that the tree was to be desired to make one wise, she took of its fruit and ate; and she also gave some to her husband, and he ate. Then the eyes of both were opened, and they knew that they were naked; and they sewed fig leaves together and made themselves aprons. (Gen. 3:1–7)

So often when people read about the serpent in Genesis their minds go back to children's Bibles that depict the serpent as a small snake slyly staring at Eve. However, in the Hebrew the word for "serpent" is *nahash*, translated as "dragon" in Isaiah 27:1 and "sea monster" in Job 26:13 (Contemporary English Version). Clearly this was an imposing foe that did not have Adam and Eve's well-being in mind.

What is important to understand is that the serpent's point of attack is not the existence of God. Rather, would Adam and Eve, created to participate in the life of the Trinity, fully enter into that life by imitating the self-donating communion of the Godhead? In short, would our original parents trust God?

Upon further study, we see that the remarks of the serpent are left unfinished. Adam and Eve must conclude the serpent's thoughts. "You will not die" if you eat the fruit, the serpent suggests. From Adam's perspective, the serpent's statement could be interpreted as a veiled threat. The enemy would kill them if they didn't eat the fruit.

Facing Adam and Eve are some choices: Would they entrust themselves to their Father, would they enter into combat with the enemy and guard the garden, would Adam defend his bride? Would Adam risk his life in a self-sacrificing offering, or would he succumb to pride and rely upon his own resources, preserving his natural life? Given Adam's awareness of the possibility of death and the veiled threat by the enemy, it is easier to see how Adam could remain silent and allow his bride to take the direct hit. And this is exactly what he did. Their disobedience resulted in death for our original parents. Adam and Eve chose to preserve their natural life, and in the process, they lost their supernatural life. Divine sonship was lost and they died spiritually. As a result, even their natural life was affected as sin ate away at their bodies and minds. Suddenly life was quite limited.

But God in His mercy would not give up on mankind. Genesis 3:15, the first announcement of good news, forecasts the day when the Messiah would crush the head of the enemy by self-donating sacrifice. The text reads, "I will put enmity between you and the woman, and between your seed and her seed; he shall bruise your head, and you shall bruise his heel." This first announcement of good news would involve a bruising, or in other words suffering.

Adam was given the opportunity to imitate the self-donating, life-giving love of the Trinity, but he failed, and the result was a curse.

> To the woman [God] said, "I will greatly multiply your pain in childbearing; in pain you shall bring forth children, yet your desire shall be for your husband, and he shall rule over you." And to Adam He said, "Because you have listened to the voice of your wife, and have eaten of the tree of which I commanded you, 'You shall not eat of it,' cursed is the ground because of you; in toil you shall eat of it all the days of your life; thorns and thistles it shall bring forth to you; and you shall eat the plants of the field. In the sweat of your face you shall eat bread till you return to the ground, for out of it you were taken; you are dust, and to dust you shall return." (Gen. 3:16–19)

The result of Adam and Eve's sin, while appearing to be devastating, would actually double as a remedial lesson, showing Adam and Eve that fruit can come out of suffering. In Genesis 3:16–19, we see that both Eve and Adam would endure suffering, but out of that suffering would come natural fruit. Eve would give herself to her husband, resulting in the pain of childbirth. The cries of childbirth would

soon turn to tears of joy, as both parents would celebrate the wonder of new life. Adam also would suffer,
and toil resulting in fruit in the form of bread from
the earth.[3]

As salvation history developed, we see that,
throughout time, God made successive covenants
with Noah, Abraham, Moses, and David. But in all
cases, man fell short of completely offering himself,
as Adam should have. If the love of the Trinity were
to be imitated in man, God would have to become a
man and face the trial that Adam faced.

The promised Messiah, Jesus Christ, became a
man two thousand years ago and fulfilled the law
(cf. Rom. 13:10) by loving the world with the
ultimate sacrifice of His life. Saint Paul calls Jesus
the "last Adam" (1 Cor. 15:20–23, 45) because He
would lay down His life "as a ransom for many"
(Mk. 10:45).

Jesus conquered death by taking on human nature,
that He "might destroy him who has the power of
death" (Heb. 2:14). He loved by freely offering
Himself for you and me and, in the process, not only
purchased us, but also set an example for us of how
to love as He loves.

The serpent in the Garden of Eden suggested to
Adam and Eve that there was an easier way to fulfill
their destiny—to grasp power by eating of the tree
of the knowledge of good and evil. The serpent's
remarks implied that one could be like God without
self-donating love. This was a lie, and Adam and Eve
bought it. Jesus faced a similar challenge in Matthew
16 when Peter suggested that Jesus could fulfill His
destiny without completely offering Himself up.

---

[3] For further reflection see Hahn, *First Comes Love*.

After giving the keys to the kingdom to Saint Peter (Mt. 16:19), Jesus announced that He was going to go to Jerusalem to suffer many things and be killed (v. 21). Peter reacts to Jesus' announcement of suffering and death with the same spirit conveyed by the serpent in the Garden of Eden, "God forbid, Lord! This shall never happen to you" (v. 22). Recognizing the false solution to the grave predicament of mankind, Jesus said, "Get behind me, Satan! You are a hindrance to me; for you are not on the side of God, but of men" (v. 23).

Before Jesus, the last Adam, moves toward the Garden of Gethsemane, Satan had already entered Judas (cf. Lk. 22:3). Jesus enters the garden (cf. Mt. 26:36), and then Judas enters the garden (cf. Jn. 18:1–3), setting up a parallel event with the Garden of Eden.

The Garden of Gethsemane scene starts out with an almost prophetic statement from Saint Peter, a statement that reflects Peter's desire to participate with Christ in His mission.

> Peter said to him, "Even if I must die with you, I will not deny you." And so said all the disciples. Then Jesus went with them to a place called Gethsemane, and he said to his disciples, "Sit here, while I go yonder and pray." And taking with him Peter and the two sons of Zebedee, he began to be sorrowful and troubled. Then he said to them, "My soul is very sorrowful, even to death; remain here, and watch with me." And going a little farther he fell on his face and prayed, "My Father, if it be possible, let this cup pass from me; nevertheless, not as I will, but as thou wilt." And he came to the disciples and found them sleeping; and he said to Peter, "So, could you not watch with me one hour? Watch and pray that you may not enter into temptation; the spirit indeed

is willing, but the flesh is weak." Again, for the second time, he went away and prayed, "My Father, if this cannot pass unless I drink it, thy will be done." And again he came and found them sleeping, for their eyes were heavy. So, leaving them again, he went away and prayed for the third time, saying the same words. Then he came to the disciples and said to them, "Are you still sleeping and taking your rest? Behold, the hour is at hand, and the Son of man is betrayed into the hands of sinners." (Mt. 26:35–45)

In the passion of Jesus, "his sweat became like great drops of blood" (Lk. 22:44), and He wore "the crown of thorns" (Jn. 19:5)—reminders of the result of Adam's ordeal (cf. Gen. 3:18–19). Jesus did what Adam should have done. "In the days of his flesh, Jesus offered up prayers and supplications, with loud cries and tears, to him who was able to save him from death, and he was heard for his godly fear. Although he was a Son, he learned obedience through what he suffered; and being made perfect he became the source of eternal salvation to all who obey him" (Heb. 5:7–9).

Though Jesus was in the form of God, He "did not count equality with God a thing to be grasped, but emptied himself, taking the form of a servant, being born in the likeness of men. And being found in human form he humbled himself and became obedient unto death, even death on a cross" (Phil. 2:5–8). Jesus completely emptied Himself and demonstrated the love of God in all its fullness. The good news is that He rose from the dead, defeating death, hell, and the grave. Indeed, Jesus answered in the affirmative the question raised in the Garden of Eden: Can we trust God? Unlike Adam, Jesus obeyed the Father and poured out His life for His bride. When we realize that the bride of Christ is the Church, and Jesus loved us so much, it's almost too much to take in. Oh, how we are loved!

But now, what about you and your suffering? Didn't Jesus suffer and die so that we wouldn't have to? Jesus suffered and died that we might become a part of the family of God, become spiritually healed and share in His nature. But He didn't eliminate suffering. The work of Christ doesn't guarantee the lack of suffering. Rather, He changed the meaning of suffering. Through baptism into Christ—into His death and Resurrection—we have become intimately joined to Him, so much so that we are His body. Because of our union with Christ, even our suffering is changed; it becomes redemptive by virtue of "being in Christ." Pope John Paul II said in his Apostolic Letter "On the Christian Meaning of Human Suffering" that "in the Cross of Christ not only is the Redemption accomplished through suffering, but *also human suffering itself has been Redeemed*."[4] In other words, suffering is worth something if it is in union with Christ.

At the point where Jesus seems to be the weakest, the complete self-donation of the Cross, the most powerful act of the Passion, the Resurrection, took place. So too, our weakness is capable of being filled with the same power manifested on the Cross. Saint Paul experienced much weakness and suffering; however, when he asked that his own infirmity be taken away, Christ answered, "My grace is sufficient for you, for my power is made perfect in weakness." Then Saint Paul could proclaim, "I will all the more gladly boast of my weaknesses, that the power of

---

[4] *Salvifici Doloris*, no. 19.

Christ may rest upon me" (2 Cor. 12:9). Pope John
Paul II, a man also acquainted with suffering, said, "It
is suffering, more than anything else, which clears the
way for the grace which transforms human souls."[5]

Saint Paul understood that our life is a cooperation with the work of Christ when he said to the
Colossians, "Now I rejoice in my sufferings for your
sake, and in my flesh I complete what is lacking in
Christ's afflictions for the sake of his body, that is,
the church" (1:24). Think about that—Paul said that
something is lacking in Christ's afflictions. What
could possibly be lacking in Christ's afflictions? Your
part! Again, Pope John Paul II said, "[T]he springs
of divine power gush forth precisely in the midst of
human weakness. Those who share in the sufferings
of Christ preserve in their own sufferings a very
special particle of the infinite treasure of the world's
Redemption, and can share this treasure with others."[6]

For the Apostle Paul, completing what is lacking
in the afflictions of Christ does not mean that the
suffering of Christ is not complete. It means that the
Redemption, accomplished through satisfactory love,
remains always open to all love expressed in human
suffering. While Jesus achieved the Redemption completely, He did not bring it to a close. The door is still
wide open to participate with Him in the redemption
of the world. We will see that our best opportunity
is during the Holy Sacrifice of the Mass where the
meaning of suffering is most clearly understood.

Jesus tells us that if we are to follow Him, we must
deny ourselves and take up our crosses daily (cf. Lk.
9:23). Our lives become an imitation and participa-

---

[5] Ibid., 27.
[6] Ibid., emphasis omitted.

tion in the love of the Trinity when we offer up our entire lives in union with Christ. "We are afflicted in every way, but not crushed; perplexed, but not driven to despair; persecuted, but not forsaken; struck down, but not destroyed; always carrying in the body the death of Jesus, so that the life of Jesus may also be manifested in our bodies. For while we live we are always being given up to death for Jesus' sake, so that the life of Jesus may be manifested in our mortal flesh. . . . [K]nowing that he who raised the Lord Jesus will raise us also with Jesus and bring us with you into his presence" (2 Cor. 4:8–11, 14).

The Resurrection is our guarantee that we can trust our heavenly Father; we can participate in the life-giving love of the Trinity by laying our lives down for the sake of His kingdom. The fruit of our suffering is raised to a supernatural level; it becomes eternal in nature. Though Eve's love for Adam resulted in suffering during childbirth, it ultimately resulted in fruit, a son. So too Jesus brought "many sons to glory . . . through suffering" (Heb. 2:10).

In the midst of suffering, we experience the love of God. We enter the very heart of the Trinity, and it is there that we come to know God. Christ allows us to participate in His Cross because that is His means of allowing us to participate in the exchanges of the Trinity, to share in the very inner life of God. This is why sometimes "bad things happen to good people." Prior to the incarnation, Mary, the mother of Jesus said "yes" to God. This "yes," her *fiat*, would result in pain. Simeon told her, "[A] sword will pierce through your own soul also" (Lk. 2:35). But what was the fruit of Mary's suffering? Life for the entire world.

As stated earlier, the suffering and death of Jesus does not mean that we won't suffer. In fact, we are told that we can expect some suffering if we follow Him. Jesus, while not removing all suffering from us, does change our suffering and makes it redemptive. Jesus empowers us with His life and enables us to love as He loves when we offer our lives in union with Him.

The most perfect place to offer our suffering in union with Christ is during the Mass. It is in the Mass that we fully participate in the mystery of Calvary. The Mass is divided into two main movements, the Liturgy of the Word and the Liturgy of the Eucharist. After the readings from Scripture and the homily, the focus shifts from the ambo to the altar. The altar is the place where the sacrifice of Jesus is offered. It's important to remember that the Paschal mystery of Christ does not remain only in the past, because He suffered and died for *all* men. This redemptive event is eternal and transcends time, making it a historically unique moment.

We participate in this unique moment by way of a sacrament. Time is mysteriously suspended, as the past, present, and future converge into the most important event in history. When we participate in the Mass, the liturgy not only recalls the events that saved us, but actualizes them in the present.

Bishop Fabian Bruskewitz in his book, *A Shepherd Speaks*, recalls a very old prayer that speaks of Mass as an *admirabile commercium*, or a "marvelous exchange."[7] Each of the two parts of the Mass is an intimate exchange with God. In the first part, the

[7] Most Rev. Fabian Bruskewitz, *A Shepherd Speaks* (San Francisco: Ignatius Press, 1997), 290–91.

Liturgy of the Word, we exchange words with God. We speak to Him in prayer and He speaks to us in His Word. In the second part, the Liturgy of the Eucharist, we bring to God our bread, wine, and offerings. These represent our work, our tears, and our joys, and yes—our suffering.

The bread used during Mass is referred to as "the host," derived from the Latin *hostia*, which means "victim." When the host is placed on the paten (usually a plate made of precious metal), it is elevated and offered to the Father by the Son. The deacon or priest pours wine into a chalice and adds a drop of water. The wine stands for Christ and the water humanity. The image here is that our humanity is totally immersed in His divinity. We truly are "in Christ."

At this point in the Mass, our attention should be completely focused on offering ourselves in union with Christ. This is the moment when our minds and hearts dare not wander. It is at this precious moment when our cares, pain, and suffering are consciously united with Christ, and we choose to love as He loved in self-donating love.

The priest invites the assembly to join him in one accord in praying "that our sacrifice may be acceptable to God, the almighty Father." While Christ is the one sacrifice on the altar, offering up their lives in union with His sacrifice unites the laity to Him.

"Then at the climax of the Mass, Christ takes our worthless gifts and changes them, through the invocation and blessing of the Holy Spirit and the words of institution, spoken by the ordained priest, into His gift of Himself to God. Thus, our gifts, joined to His, become of infinite worth and of unsurpassable value. This is what makes each Mass, even when imperfect with defective music, ceremonies, rubrics or homily, infinitely meritorious before God."[8]

The great exchange has taken place, and all things have become new, and "in everything God works for good for those who love him, who are called according to His purpose" (Rom. 8:28). Indeed, when we participate with Christ by offering our lives in sacrificial union with Him, we enter the heart of the Trinity and can truly say, "I have come to know His love."

Are you suffering now? Do not despair—this is your opportunity to draw close to Christ and entrust yourself to God (cf. 1 Pet. 2:23; 4:19). By picking up your cross and following Christ, you will come to know Him more deeply. Each of us should leave the celebration of the Mass knowing that we have found and participated in the meaning of suffering. Armed with this knowledge of the nature of suffering, we can go through anything and need not despair.

What is the worst thing that has ever happened on earth? Deicide—the crucifixion of God. What was the result? The salvation of the world. If God brought such a great good out of such evil, then what can He bring out of your situation?

Having returned to the Catholic Church after twelve years as a Protestant pastor, Jeff Cavins communicates his zeal and deep love for Jesus Christ with clarity and enthusiasm through radio, television, books, and conferences.

CHAPTER XII

A Marriage Made in Heaven
Eucharistic and Marital Communion

KIMBERLY HAHN

People arrive early to finalize the decorations, tune their instruments, or assist the bridal party. The anticipation of those gathered grows by the moment as first the mother of the bride, then the mother of the groom, and finally the groom and his men appear. The music echoes the expectant atmosphere, as bridesmaid after bridesmaid proceeds down the aisle until the flower girl and ring bearer begin their promenade. As the little ones reach the altar area, the music changes, the mother of the bride stands—and all with her—turning to glimpse father and daughter enter the back of the church.

The radiant bride gently holds her father's arm as they glide up the aisle. The groom stands in amazement of the gift with which he is about to be presented. Was there ever a time she was more beautiful? Was there ever a time he was more grateful? The glory of the bride is the glory of the groom.

This is the long-awaited moment—the transition from her father's side into her groom's arms. This is the fulfillment of myriad dreams, the answer to innumerable prayers, the transition from two families to a new family. Though a relatively common occurrence, this is a miracle.

Each wedding ceremony gives us a glimpse into a deeper understanding of the love of the Bridegroom of our soul, Jesus, and our role as His Bride, the Church. The bride's grand entrance, her radiant countenance, her pure white gown that covers her—all inspire thoughts of the beauty of Jesus' Bride, the Church, when she will be presented to her Groom in all of her splendor.

The sacrament of Matrimony is a celebration of the union of two persons and the communion they share. Likewise, the Mass is a celebration of the union of two persons and the communion we share. The Scriptures reveal ways in which both the sacraments of Matrimony and the Eucharist are mutually illuminating. We see this especially when we consider that Jesus' first miracle took place at a wedding in Cana where He transformed water into wine (Jn. 2), and when we consider the culmination of history in the marriage supper of the Lamb (Rev. 19).

Let's take a look at the elements of the Rite of Marriage, as celebrated in the context of the Mass, and see some of the comparisons between the two sacraments of union and communion: Matrimony and the Eucharist.[1]

---

[1] All statements in bold are quotations from the "Rite for Celebrating Marriage during Mass" in John F. Kippley, *Marriage Is for Keeps: Foundations for Christian Marriage* (Cincinnati, OH: Foundation for the Family, 1994), 115–161.

The Penitential Rite—
Preparing to Receive One Another

Before a couple declares their love publicly, they develop their relationship privately. They have to get to know each other before they can "know" each other in the biblical sense (cf. Gen. 4:1). Though most married couples acknowledge that a lifetime is not enough time to sufficiently know each other, a courting couple must know each other well enough to consent freely and fully to give themselves to the other.

They also need to learn how to disagree agreeably, an art in any relationship. Confession (both interpersonal and sacramental) precedes intimacy, as they will soon discover in their married life; when one (or both) has sinned against the other, harmony is disrupted and intimacy is blocked. Asking each other and the Lord for forgiveness restores harmony and prepares for intimacy.

Likewise, Confession precedes our intimacy with our Lord in the Eucharist. Our sin blocks the channel of grace; Confession clears the channel so that grace can flow, restoring harmony in our relationship with God. When we approach our Lord in the Eucharist, we want to receive all of the grace He has for us. To receive Him worthily and fruitfully, we need to be prepared.

Opening Prayer

After the Penitential Rite, the celebrant prays for the couple.

Here are two samples:

> Lord, you have made the bond of marriage a holy
> mystery, a symbol of Christ's love for his Church. . . .
> With faith in you and in each other they pledge their
> love today. May their lives always bear witness to the
> reality of that love.

Or

> Father, when you created mankind you willed that
> man and wife should be one. Bind N. and N. in the
> loving union of marriage; and make their love fruitful
> so that they may be living witnesses to your divine
> love in the world.

These prayers highlight the fact that the wedding ceremony is more than a public event joining two lives;
it's a liturgical ceremony joining two persons rooted
in faith in Christ. First, they were consecrated individually to God; now they are giving their faith-filled
lives to each other. Consequently, they are presenting
the holy gift of themselves to each other.

The wedding is far more than a service to acknowledge the couple's love; it is a commissioning of the
couple to witness to the world God's divine love for
the world. They have been created for love; through
this vocation to love, their fruitfulness will be a part
of their testimony to the world of God's love.

Each beautiful expression of human love points us
back to God; for "'God is love' (1 Jn. 4:8) and in himself he lives a mystery of personal loving communion."[2]
God created man, male and female, in love and called
them to love as He does—with total self-giving. Once
sin entered the world through the consent of Adam

---

[2] Pontifical Council for the Family, *The Truth and Meaning of Human
Sexuality: Guidelines for Education within the Family* (November 21,
1995), no. 8.

and Eve, they began to struggle with selfishness and conditional love. God, however, restores us through the self-giving love of Christ. It is this gift of Christ's self-offering that we receive through the Eucharist. We continue to struggle with selfishness, but we also receive grace to help us become less selfish.

Just as a wedding ceremony is a public declaration of love and fidelity to the beloved, so the Mass is a public declaration of our fidelity to the Beloved of our soul. We bear testimony to our Faith and to the One in whom we place our trust.

Liturgy of the Word—Old Testament Reading

One of the most common Old Testament readings, used in the wedding Mass, is Genesis 1:26–28, 31:

> God said, "Let us make man in our image, after our likeness; . . ." So God created man in his own image, in the image of God he created him; male and female he created them. And God blessed them, and God said to them, "Be fruitful and multiply, and fill the earth and subdue it; and have dominion. . . ." And God saw everything that he had made, and behold, it was very good.

Unlike any other creature God made, man and woman were uniquely created in the image and likeness of God. The communion of Triune love—Father, Son and Holy Spirit—called man and woman into existence and blessed their union in marriage.

God created man and woman with the capacity of loving, interpersonal communion with God and with each other. As the *Catechism* says, "Being in the image of God the human individual possesses the dignity of a person, capable of self-knowledge, of self-possession, and of freely giving himself and entering into communion with other persons. And he is called by grace to a covenant with his Creator, to offer him a response of faith and love that no other creature can give in his stead" (no. 357). Therefore, man and woman were given the responsibility of loving, interpersonal communion with God and with each other. This is the reason that God's first command is also their nuptial blessing: they are to be fruitful and multiply. Their love was never intended to be self-absorbing, but to be self-donating, and therefore life-giving.

The Father, Son, and Holy Spirit withhold nothing from each other. Their love reflects total self-donation. It is to this kind of generous self-donation that each man and woman, especially within the sacrament of Marriage, is called to imitate.

We see a human expression of the self-donating love of the Trinity in Jesus' self-offering on the Cross. There was no limit to the self-donation He was willing to make on our behalf. Unlike the first Adam's failure to lay down his life for his bride in the garden, Jesus laid down His life for His Bride, the Church. It is this very life, given up for us on the Cross and then taken up in Resurrection and Ascension to glory, that is offered to us in each Mass.

Another common Old Testament reading for the ceremony is Genesis 2:18–24.

> [T]he LORD God said, "It is not good that the man should be alone; I will make him a helper fit for him." So out of the ground the LORD God formed every beast of the field and every bird of the air, and brought them to the man to see what he would call them . . . but for the man there was not found a

helper fit for him. So the LORD God caused a deep
sleep to fall upon the man, and while he slept took
one of his ribs and closed up its place with flesh; and
the rib which the LORD God had taken from the man
he made into a woman and brought her to the man.
Then the man said, "This at last is bone of my bones
and flesh of my flesh; she shall be called Woman,
because she was taken out of Man." Therefore a man
leaves his father and his mother and cleaves to his
wife, and they become one flesh.

Throughout the creation account, God declares
everything to be good until this statement, "It is not
good that the man should be alone" (Gen. 2:18).
Man is good, but the fact that he is alone is not. The
Lord wants to give the man a helpmate, a partner, an
intimate companion, and no other creature would
do. Woman is uniquely created for man; she completes him.

Immediately the man recognizes the gift that the
woman is for him. Filled with gratitude, he exclaims
that she is the fulfillment of his desire to be united in
love. This is not just a meeting of minds, but a union
of flesh. Their one-flesh expression of love is a sign
of their new family bond.

The wedding ceremony functions as a formal
"leaving and cleaving" for the couple. Though there is
a sense in which each family gains a new family member, there is also a new family formed. From this time
forth, whether or not children become part of the
family, this new couple constitutes a new family unit.

The Mass illustrates this truth in its spiritual
dimension: When we receive the Body and Blood
of Jesus, our flesh is united to His. We are enjoying
interpersonal communion. When we receive Jesus,
we not only enjoy a relationship with Him, but we

acknowledge our place within the family of God. We have a family bond: His Father is our Father, His mother becomes our mother, and His brothers and sisters in the Church become our brothers and sisters.

Responsorial Psalm

The Psalms have a number of themes appropriate for the celebration of a wedding. In Psalms 34:1–8, the psalmist invites the people to bless the Lord, to praise Him for His steadfast love, to be thankful for His many blessings and to exalt the Lord's name. Why? The psalmist says the Lord has heard his cries for help, delivered him from foes, preserved his life, and offered him refuge. This passage reminds all in attendance at the wedding of the ways in which the Lord has faithfully answered their prayers.

Reflecting on the past is one of the best ways to prepare for future challenges. Not only has the Lord abundantly provided in the past, but He will most assuredly provide all that this young couple requires as they begin their life as a new family.

The closing sentence of this passage, "O taste and see that the Lord is good! Happy is the man who takes refuge in him" (34:8), has two meanings. Figuratively, it is an invitation to reflect on the goodness of the Lord in our lives with gratitude. Literally, we are to receive the Lord in the Eucharist, thankful for his good gift.

Another favorite responsorial psalm for the wedding Mass is Psalms 103:1–2, 8, 13, 17–18a. Its primary theme is the kindness and mercy of the Lord. It closes with this thought, "But the steadfast love of the LORD is from everlasting to everlasting upon those who fear him, and his righteousness to children's children, to those who keep his covenant and remember to do his commandments."

God's covenant faithfulness is the basis of our faith. The wedding in the context of the Mass is itself a demonstration of God's covenant faithfulness, for in many cases, we have the grandparents and parents witnessing the vows of their children in the same context—a Mass—in which they themselves began their marital unions. God has been faithful to those who fear them. Further, the Lord will extend His faithfulness to the next generation. As the author of Proverbs writes, "In the fear of the LORD one has strong confidence, and his children will have a refuge" (Prov. 14:26).

The Lord declares His covenantal faithfulness to Joshua following the death of Moses, "[A]s I was with Moses, so I will be with you; I will not fail you or forsake you. Be strong and of good courage" (Josh. 1:5b–6a). These words are quoted in Hebrews immediately after the author commands faithfulness in marriage: "Let marriage be held in honor among all, and let the marriage bed be undefiled; for God will judge the immoral and adulterous. Keep your life free from love of money, and be content with what you have; for he has said, 'I will never fail you nor forsake you'" (Heb. 13:4, 5). The Lord's covenantal faithfulness is the basis for our faithfulness to our marriage covenant. We have His word that He will never forsake us; likewise we must give our word that we will never forsake our beloved.

Jesus' gift of Himself to us in the Mass is another expression of His covenantal faithfulness. He will never leave us; He will never forsake us. When we receive the Lord in the Eucharist, we are strengthened in our resolve to be faithful to the Lord and to be faithful in our vocation.

New Testament Reading

The New Testament reading directly addresses the couple marrying. One possible reading is Romans 12:1–2, 9–18. Verse one states, "I appeal to you, therefore, brethren, by the mercies of God, to present your bodies as a living sacrifice, holy and acceptable to God, which is your spiritual worship." This passage summarizes two of the most difficult concepts to fully grasp when young people marry.

The first difficult concept is our call to be a living sacrifice. A couple preparing for marriage has confidence that no sacrifice will be too great for one person to make for the other. Love is strong and able to overcome any difficulty. However, it's not necessarily the great sacrifices that are as difficult to offer to the Lord, as much as the small sacrifices we have to make daily.

Saint Paul makes it clear that sacrificial living involves our bodies and not just our minds or our spirits. This sacrificial living is a physical act of our spiritual worship. And it can only be done by the mercy of God—we do not have the inner strength to be living sacrifices on our own. Thankfully, God never asks us to do it on our own.

One of the most beautiful ways we offer ourselves as living sacrifices is through the gift of new life. In fact, the Pontifical Council on the Family, reflecting on the words of Pope John Paul II, says, "The revealing sign of authentic married love is openness to Life . . . '[Conjugal love] makes them capable of the greatest possible gift, the gift by which they become cooperators with God for giving life to a new human person . . . a living reflection of their love, a permanent sign of conjugal unity and a living and inseparable synthesis of their being a father and a mother' [*Familiaris Consortio*, no. 14]."[3] Children embody our love.

It's one thing to consent to the idea of being open to life; it's quite another to go through weeks of queasy feelings, nights of interrupted sleep to go to the bathroom, and months of changing body dimensions, including a few stretch marks here and there. No matter how the child arrives on the scene, whether through natural childbirth or C-section, both kinds of deliveries are fraught with challenge, danger, and pain. However, the joy of bearing a new life into the world overcomes all difficulties.

When a man and woman conceive a child, they become a father and a mother. As they embrace the gift of each other, they become cooperators with God in the supreme gift of marriage—a new life. Self-donation expresses life-giving love. Love leads to life; life leads to sacrifice.

Our lives change with each new life that enters our union, no matter how brief that life may be (as a consequence of miscarriage or stillbirth). Our communion of love is an expression of the civilization of love—two persons now reflect the Trinitarian love of three Persons. We savor the unspeakable privilege that is ours, to reflect the image and likeness of God, when we gaze on our own image and likeness reflected in a son or daughter.

Through these sacrificial offerings, we can say, "I have been crucified with Christ; it is no longer I

---

[3] Ibid., no. 15.

who live, but Christ who lives in me. And the life I
now live in the flesh I live by faith in the Son of God
who loved me and gave himself for me" (Gal. 2:20).
We are able to give ourselves to this incredible degree
because we have a Lord who has given far more to us.
He has withheld nothing from us; now He asks us to
do the same.

We also have the assurance that the sufferings we
experience have redemptive value because of the sufferings of Christ. Saint Paul says, "Now I rejoice in my
sufferings for your sake, and in my flesh I complete
what is lacking in Christ's afflictions for the sake of
his body, that is, the church" (Col. 1:24). What does
Saint Paul mean? Surely there's nothing incomplete
about Christ's sacrifice. However, Saint Paul demon-
strates how Christ's suffering is completed: since we
are a part of His body, our sufferings, united to His,
are a participation in Christ's self-offering.

At each Mass we reflect on the sacrificial offering
of Christ on our behalf. It is an unbloody sacrifice,
yet it recalls the very real humiliation, suffering and
death of our Lord. At the same time, it also recalls His
victory over death and the fear of death. All of this
puts our sufferings in context: our suffering cannot
compare to Christ's, yet it is His suffering that makes
ours meaningful.

Romans 12:2 continues, "Do not be conformed
to this world but be transformed by the renewal of
your mind, that you may prove what is the will of
God, what is good and acceptable and perfect." Most
of us do not realize the extent to which our current
culture attempts to mold our thinking. We are indoc-
trinated through all forms of media and educated in
schools to see men and women as objects to be used,

rather than people to be honored and respected. We are coaxed into seeing marriage as an outdated institution in favor of cohabitation. We are mocked for imagining we can remain virgins before marriage or retain faithfulness within marriage. We are ridiculed for having more than 2.1 children, as if we are damaging the environment or living selfishly. We cannot resist conforming to these lies unless we fill our hearts and minds with truth.

For us to resist the temptation to be conformed to this world, we have to follow Saint Paul's advice: "[B]e transformed by the renewal of your mind." Since marriage is God's idea in the first place, we need to find out how He wants us to live married life. After all, no one gets married in the hopes of failing. If we want to succeed, let's try to do God's will God's way.

Thankfully, the Church is eager to instruct us, if we will take the time to listen. One of our best resources is the *Catechism of the Catholic Church*. Hopefully, through pre-Cana classes, parishes will offer couples these resources as well as clear scriptural teaching, so that they will renew their minds about what it means to be a husband or a wife, a father or a mother.

Families are called to be generous in their love of life, being open to accept the children the Lord wants to give them. Pope John Paul II addressed this in his first trip to the United States in 1979, "It is certainly less serious to deny their children certain comforts or material advantages than to deprive them of the presence of brothers and sisters, who could help them to grow in humanity and to realize the beauty of life at all its ages and in all its variety."[4]

---

[4] John Paul II, "Homily at Capitol Hill," in *L'Osservatore Romano*, November 5, 1979.

In *Humanae Vitae* (a document that all married couples would do well to read), Pope Paul VI calls married couples to "responsible parenthood," which "corresponds to the will of God the Creator" (*HV* 10). He points out the boundaries that will safeguard the sanctity of the act of marriage. While emphasizing that families are called to be generous in their openness to life, Pope Paul recognizes that "if . . . there are well-grounded reasons for spacing births, arising from the physical or psychological condition of husband or wife, or from external circumstances, the Church teaches that married people may then take advantage of the natural cycles immanent in the reproductive system . . . , thus controlling birth in a way which does not in the least offend the moral principle" (*HV* 16). He also reiterates the perennial teaching of the Church that "sexual intercourse which is deliberately contraceptive . . . [is] intrinsically wrong" (*HV* 14). He warns us of the consequences of this serious sin: our communion with the Lord is broken and the interpersonal communion between husband and wife damaged.

To generously live their vocation, married couples need to seek continually the help of God, especially by "draw[ing] grace and charity from that unfailing fount which is the Eucharist" (*HV* 25).

This renewal of the mind is an ongoing process— each Mass is a part of this renewal. The Liturgy of the Word teaches us more and more about what it means to live as a child of God, including many applications to married life. In addition, the Liturgy of the Eucharist inspires us through the example of Christ to want to follow Him in generous, sacrificial love. Our minds and our hearts are challenged.

The remaining verses of Romans 12:9–18 are similar to the admonitions in another reading, Colossians 3:12–17:

> Put on then, as God's chosen ones, holy and beloved, compassion, kindness, lowliness, meekness, and patience, forbearing one another and, if one has a complaint against another, forgiving each other; as the Lord has forgiven you, so you also must forgive. And above all these put on love, which binds everything together in perfect harmony. And let the peace of Christ rule in your hearts, to which indeed you were called in the one body. And be thankful. Let the word of Christ dwell in you richly, teach and admonish one another in all wisdom, and sing psalms and hymns and spiritual songs with thankfulness in your hearts to God. And whatever you do, in word or deed, do everything in the name of the Lord Jesus, giving thanks to God the Father through him.

Here are the keys to unlock a successful marriage and family. Not only does the Church recommend this passage for weddings, but she also focuses our attention on this passage every year on the feast of the Holy Family.

What are the essential traits of a marriage made in heaven? First, the couple needs to be able to give and receive forgiveness. The perfect marriage is not without sin. Rather, it's a relationship rooted in grace: in the grace shown each of us by Christ so that we can be called holy and beloved ones, and in the grace we show each other. Kindness, forbearance, patience, humility and compassion are the virtues we foster so that we are channels of grace. We allow love to cover a multitude of sins.

Thankfulness is another essential trait of a godly marriage. We fill our hearts with thanksgiving for our spouse. Of course, we see weaknesses and sins in each other, but each day we choose to focus on our spouse's gifts, abilities, talents, virtues, and personal strengths. We cultivate a heart of gratitude and contentment rather than a critical and contentious spirit.

We have been called to be a people characterized by thankfulness—a Eucharistic people. (The Greek word *eucharisteo* means "I give thanks.") When we assist at Mass, we give thanks for the incredible gift we have received through Jesus. We acknowledge the Giver and the gift. Rather than expressing a critical spirit toward the priest, choir, or other people in attendance, we focus on our relationship with the Lord and the unspeakable blessing of being in His presence and receiving Him into our very being.

When we choose to give thanks for the gift of the person we are receiving, whether the Lord or our spouse, we are freer to love that person. Living in love requires more than an initial decision—it is a daily choice to give our lives to our Lord and to our spouse. Thankfulness cements our faithfulness to both.

Another New Testament passage suggested for a wedding Mass is Ephesians 5:21–33.

> Be subject to one another out of reverence for Christ. Wives, be subject to your husbands, as to the Lord. For the husband is the head of the wife as Christ is the head of the church, his body, and is himself its Savior. As the church is subject to Christ, so let wives also be subject in everything to their husbands. Husbands, love your wives, as Christ loved the church and gave himself up for her, that he might

sanctify her, having cleansed her by the washing of water with the word, that he might present the church to himself in splendor, without spot or wrinkle or any such thing, that she might be holy and without blemish. Even so husbands should love their wives as their own bodies. He who loves his wife loves himself. For no man ever hates his own flesh, but nourishes and cherishes it, as Christ does the church, because we are members of his body. "For this reason a man shall leave his father and mother and be joined to his wife, and the two shall become one flesh." This is a great mystery, and I mean in reference to Christ and the church; however, let each one of you love his wife as himself, and let the wife see that she respects her husband.

In this passage, Saint Paul highlights some of the ways Christian marriage is its own witness to the world of the relationship between Christ and the Church.

First, there is an authority structure, rooted in mutual submission to Christ of both husband and wife, for a harmonious relationship—husbands are the head of the family just as Christ is the head of His bride, the Church. Note that Saint Paul immediately addresses the concern about what kind of authority might be wielded: husbands are to lead by laying down their lives for their wives, just as Christ has sacrificed Himself for His bride. This is a call to radical self-donation, to servant leadership.

Husbands are to cherish their wives as much as their own bodies, to nourish their wives emotionally and spiritually, and to see themselves as belonging to their wives in a one-flesh union. Likewise, wives are to respect their husbands and to love them in imitation of their husband's sacrificial love, just as the Bride of Christ imitates the sacrificial love of Christ.

At each Mass, we remember of the sacrificial offering of our Lord on our behalf. We know our privileged position as the bride of Christ. We approach
our Groom with awe and reverence as we prepare to
receive Him as gift. We acknowledge the authority
He has as our Lord, and the derivative authority He
has given to His Bride, the Church.

Each of our marriages, by the grace of God, can
be a living example of the mystery of Christ's nuptial
relationship to the Church. Through our faithfulness
and fruitfulness, we are a witness to the covenant
between God and man. And each Mass bears testimony to the covenantal faithfulness and fruitfulness God
is reproducing in His Bride, the Church.

Gospel

For the Gospel selection, a couple may choose
Matthew 7:21, 24–29:

> Not every one who says to me, "Lord, Lord," shall
> enter the kingdom of heaven, but he who does the
> will of my Father who is in heaven. . . . Every one
> then who hears these words of mine and does them
> will be like a wise man who built his house upon the
> rock; and the rain fell, and the floods came, and the
> winds blew and beat upon that house, but it did not
> fall, because it had been founded on the rock. And
> every one who hears these words of mine and does
> not do them will be like a foolish man who built
> his house upon the sand; and the rain fell, and the
> floods came, and the winds blew and beat against
> that house, and it fell; and great was the fall of it.

How will we build our home (family)? On sand or on
rock? To build a solid family is to do the will of our
heavenly Father in our family. It's not enough to say
Jesus is the Lord, if we do not follow Him. Storms

in life will come; there's no stopping them. We can withstand them, however, if our foundation is solid.

Not only is Jesus the rock—the cornerstone which the builders rejected—but He established the Church as a foundation of truth in our lives. The Church calls us to allow our mutual love to be truly self-donating in a life-giving way. "The revealing sign of authentic married love is openness to life."[5] Marriage makes the couple capable to receive "the greatest possible gift, the gift by which they become cooperators with God for giving life to a new human person . . . a living reflection of their love, a permanent sign of conjugal unity and a living and inseparable synthesis of their being a father and a mother."[6] What a glorious vision for the meaning of the act of marriage!

Yet this vision is frequently assailed. One of the storms a marriage faces is challenges to openness to life. We may begin marriage with a conviction to be open to life, but then financial concerns creep in, or people criticize us for not using contraception, or we experience a miscarriage or stillbirth, and we question whether or not we can continue live this teaching. Is this teaching more of an ideal to be sought than a truth to be lived?[7]

No, by the grace of God, the Church's teaching on openness to life can and must be lived. The unitive and procreative aspects of the act of marriage cannot be separated without serious sin resulting. The Church frequently reminds us that "[t]his happens

---

[5] *The Truth and Meaning of Human Sexuality*, no. 15.
[6] Ibid.
[7] See my book, *Life-Giving Love: Embracing God's Beautiful Design for Marriage* (Ann Arbor, MI: Charis, 2001), for a more thorough examination of common objections and answers to the Church's vision regarding openness to life.

above all in contraception and artificial procreation. In the first case, one intends to seek sexual pleasure, intervening in the conjugal act to avoid conception; in the second case conception is sought by substituting the conjugal act with a technique. These are actions contrary to the truth of married love and contrary to full communion between husband and wife."[8] We are meant to enjoy this beautiful act of self-donating love in the act of marriage, fully embracing the other, including each other's fertility.

Another Gospel account frequently read at weddings is Matthew 19:3–6:

> And Pharisees came up to him and tested him by asking, "Is it lawful to divorce one's wife for any cause?" He answered, "Have you not read that he who made them from the beginning made them male and female, and said, 'For this reason a man shall leave his father and mother and be joined to his wife, and the two shall become one flesh'? So they are no longer two but one flesh. What therefore God has joined together, let not man put asunder."

Marriage is God's business—He is the one who unites husband and wife and makes them one flesh. Man cannot undo what God has done. The two have become one. This is how He established marriage; this is how He maintains marriage.

Children are the embodiment of marital love. They are the quintessential example of the indissolubility of marriage—how can we ever separate a child back into the parts that each person contributed? Likewise, there is an indissoluble bond between the Church and Jesus Christ.

---

[8] *The Truth and Meaning of Human Sexuality*, no. 32.

Another Gospel account for a wedding is John 15:12–17:

> This is my commandment, that you love one another as I have loved you. Greater love has no man than this, that a man lay down his life for his friends. You are my friends if you do what I command you. No longer do I call you servants, for the servant does not know what his master is doing; but I have called you friends, for all that I have heard from my Father I have made known to you. You did not choose me, but I chose you and appointed you that you should go and bear fruit and that your fruit should abide; so that whatever you ask the Father in my name, he may give it to you. This I command you, to love one another.

As wonderful as the love between two people can be, it has to go deeper than romantic love. It has to be the kind of deeply sacrificial love reflecting Christ's love for each of them. Jesus said, "Love one another as I have loved you." He calls us to imitate the love the Father and Son have for each other.

The Lord has chosen this couple to enter into the covenant of marriage. He has chosen them to bear fruit that lasts. Loving one another as the Lord has loved them is foundational for a marriage and family that will last. This is the kind of love in which children should be conceived and nurtured.

The command to love one another in imitation of Jesus is also given in the broader context to the whole Church. When we gather before the Eucharist, we are reminded what the cost of so great a love is—total self-donation. There is nothing that our Lord has withheld from us; we are to imitate the Bridegroom of our soul and withhold nothing from Him. Then we are to love each other in the Body of Christ just as the head of the Body has loved us.

Statement of Intentions

The priest asks the Lord to seal and strengthen the love of the new husband and wife in the presence of the witnesses, the priest and community. **"Christ abundantly blesses this love. He has already consecrated you in baptism and now he enriches and strengthens you by a special sacrament so that you may assume the duties of marriage in mutual and lasting fidelity."** Then the priest invites "the spouses, as ministers of Christ's grace, [to] mutually confer upon each other the sacrament of Matrimony by expressing their consent before the Church" (*Catechism*, no. 1623).

Bride and groom profess in front of the assembled witnesses that they are entering into this union freely and without reservation. They state their desire to serve and honor each other as long as both shall live. And they accept, as God's special blessing, any children God gives them, along with the commitment to educate them. Their marriage vow is all-encompassing: for better or for worse, for richer or for poorer, in sickness and in health, to love and honor all the days of their lives. This profession demands faithfulness.

Christ, through the sacraments, strengthens us to be faithful. When we make our reception of the Eucharist a priority, and when we make regular use of Confession, we are strengthened individually *and* as a married couple. Our pledges of faithfulness are necessary, but we need the Holy Spirit to seal those pledges, to add His faithfulness to our own.

Blessing and Exchange of Rings: Sign of Love and Fidelity

The rings the bride and groom exchange are more than pieces of jewelry. They symbolize the couple's love for and commitment to the other. They are a sign to others that the couple have pledged their lives each other; the two have become yoked.

The Eucharist is a reminder of the faithfulness of God, day in, day out. It is a pledge between Christ and His Church to give their lives completely to one another. And it is a sign of full communion to those outside the Church.

Prayer of the Faithful

Prayers are offered for the pope as he leads the whole Church, for the Church and political leaders to strengthen family life, for the beloved relatives of the couple, both living and dead, and for any special intentions the couple may have. Prayer is the breath of the soul and the life-blood of a marriage. Prayer takes place throughout the wedding just as it needs to occur throughout the marriage.

Our life of prayer within the family is so important. We have many occasions to draw our family together in prayer. We rejoice with each other on birthdays and our parents' anniversaries, holidays and Holy Days—these special times are causes for praise and thanksgiving to the Lord. Likewise, we can bear each other's burdens in times of sadness or difficulty through prayer when there is a loss of a job or a child, marital stress, or financial challenges. We teach our children to go to God in prayer by bringing their young hearts before Him regularly.

The Mass, likewise, is a prayer. We pray the Mass, offering ourselves through the gift of bread and wine. The Holy Spirit transforms the bread and the wine into the Body, Blood, Soul and Divinity of our Lord, so that we might receive Jesus Himself. We are able to worship and adore the Lord of lords in the Eucharist. And we spend time in thanksgiving after receiving our Lord.

Liturgy of the Eucharist

The priest prays at the beginning of the Liturgy of the Eucharist: **"Today you have made them one in the sacrament of marriage. May the mystery of Christ's unselfish love, which we celebrate in this [E]ucharist, increase their love for you and for each other."** Jesus' love for His Bride, the Church, inspires the hearts of bride and groom alike to imitate Him.

There is something particularly fitting for a bride and groom to celebrate their wedding in the context of the Mass; they are giving themselves completely to each other as a gift, just as Christ has done for them. And the gift is ongoing, just as Christ continually offers Himself both to the Father in Heaven and on the altar each day in the Eucharist. By "communicating in the same Body and the same Blood of Christ, they may form but 'one body' in Christ [cf. 1 Cor. 10:17]" (*Catechism*, no. 1621). Intimacy with Christ increases intimacy as a couple.

The Eucharistic Prayer includes these phrases:

> **By this sacrament your grace unites man and woman in an unbreakable bond of love and peace. You have designed the chaste love of husband and wife for the increase both of the human family and**

of your own family born in baptism. . . . In Christian marriage you bring together the two orders of creation: nature's gift of children enriches the world and your grace enriches also your Church.

Or

You created man in love to share your divine life. We see this high destiny in the love of husband and wife, which bears the imprint of your own divine love. Love is man's origin, love is his constant calling, love is his fulfillment in heaven. The love of man and woman is made holy in the sacrament of marriage, and becomes the mirror of your everlasting love.

The Church continually reminds the bride and groom that their relationship is not a closed circle. By the very nature of their love, they are called to be life-giving lovers. And their generosity of love and life will not only enrich their family, but the family of God in the Church as well. Their love reflects the Father's love; their love is not an end in itself, but a way of sharing divine love and divine life. Their love points beyond themselves in the present to its greatest fulfillment in heaven.

The Nuptial Blessing

The nuptial blessing follows the Lord's Prayer.

Father, by your power you have made everything out of nothing. In the beginning you created the universe and made mankind in your own likeness. You gave man the constant help of woman so that man and woman should no longer be two, but one flesh, and you teach us that what you have united may never be

divided. Father, you have made the union of man
and wife so holy a mystery that it symbolizes the
marriage of Christ and his Church. Father, by your
plan man and woman are united, and married life
has been established as the one blessing that was
not forfeited by original sin or washed away in the
flood.

Or

Holy Father, you created mankind in your own
image and made man and woman to be joined as
husband and wife in union of body and heart and
so fulfill their mission in this world. Father, to
reveal the plan of your love, you made the union
of husband and wife an image of the covenant
between you and your people. In the fulfillment of
this sacrament, the marriage of Christian man and
woman is a sign of the marriage between Christ
and the Church. . . . Father, grant that as they come
together to your table on earth, so they may one
day have the joy of sharing your feast in heaven.

Human love is both physical and spiritual. "In
marriage the physical intimacy of the spouses
becomes a sign and pledge of spiritual communion"
(*Catechism*, no. 2360). Married life is the one blessing that still exists from before the Fall. Husband and
wife, by loving and honoring each other faithfully in
the covenant of marriage, are a sign to the world of
Christ's relationship to His Church.

The nuptial meaning of the body refers to our
capacity to be a gift to another person and to receive
another person as gift. When human sexuality within
marriage properly expresses this giving and receiving
the other as gift, both husband and wife experience
the dignity of being treated as persons. Wherever
self-donating love is given, the civilization of love

grows. When they embrace children as the fruit of their love, the civilization of life-giving love expands. This is a significant way in which we image the Trinity who called us into existence; for Holy Communion is a communion with the Father, Son and Holy Spirit, the ultimate civilization of love from which all other expressions of communion find their identity.

In contrast, when the focus of the act of marriage is self-gratification, both partners use each other, reducing the other to an object. This produces "a civilization in which persons are used in the same way as things are used. In the context of a civilization of use, woman can become an object for man, children hindrance to parents." This becomes the civilization of death.

The bride and groom's invitation to the Lord's table anticipates the life-long communion they will share in Christ. Their communion on earth is a pre-cursor to their invitation to the marriage supper of the Lamb in heaven. Both the sacraments of Marriage and Eucharist encourage a future orientation: this life is short, and we are to live it in light of eternity.

How is it possible to live this vocation to love like Christ in the vocation of marriage and in the Church? It is only possible by the power of the Holy Spirit. We are transformed by the presence of the Holy Spirit within us through Baptism. We are sealed in the Holy Spirit through Confirmation. We are strengthened by the Holy Spirit through the grace of Reconciliation. We are given the Eucharist through the Holy Spirit's transformation of bread and wine into Christ. And we are united by the Spirit in Holy Matrimony. "The Holy Spirit is the seal of their covenant, the

ever-available source of their love and the strength to
renew their fidelity" (*Catechism*, no. 1624).

Sign of Peace

The sign of peace is a time where the new husband and wife share Christ's peace with their new
families as well as their original families. Christ is
the source of all peace. Christ brings His peace to the
world in the Eucharist, through His Church. We then
become channels of peace.

Communion

Communion is the time of supreme intimacy with
our Lord. Just as the bride comes up the aisle to greet
her beloved, so we come forward to receive the Lover
of our soul. Out of the great love with which He has
loved us, He condescends not only to fill our hearts
but also to have us receive Him into our bodies. As
He promised, "Behold, I stand at the door and knock;
if anyone opens the door, I will come into him and eat
with him, and he with me" (Rev. 3:20). This time of
intimacy with our Lord prepares us for intimacy with
our spouse.

Prayer after Communion

The priest concludes the service with a prayer and
a blessing: "**Lord, in your love you have given us this
[E]ucharist to unite us with one another and with you.
As you have made N. and N. one in this sacrament
of marriage (and in the sharing of the one bread and
the one cup), so now make them one in love for each
other.**" Christ's love for the couple is the source of
their unity. "This human communion is confirmed,
purified, and completed by communion in Jesus

Christ, given through the sacrament of Matrimony. It is deepened by lives of the common faith and by the Eucharist received together" (*Catechism*, no. 1644). Union flows from communion.

The final blessing includes a request for the peace of Christ to rule in their home, for the blessing of children, for true friends to assist the couple, and for the couple to be a clear witness to the world of God's love for the poor and needy. The priest concludes with, **"But may your hearts' first desire be always the good things waiting for you in the life of heaven."**

In other words, the couple has been blessed to be a blessing. It's not just about the two of them—their marriage is placed in the larger context of the mission of the Church and the needs of the world. Their marriage is a sign that points beyond them to God's intimate union with his people. And the couple is to go forth from their wedding Mass—as we leave every Mass—"to love and to serve the Lord."

Thanksgiving and celebration follows the wedding Mass. There is such joy for the couple as they rejoice with family and friends. And later, as they share physical intimacy, they can be naked without shame. They experience the deep peace that follows such intimacy, resting in the arms of the beloved who has now been consecrated for him or her alone.

Similarly, following the Mass, we thank God for the One we have just received. There's time for silent reflection, relishing the renewal of our covenant with our Lord, savoring the Savior, grateful for deep contentment that flows from intimate communion with our Lord.

Conclusion

What a gift our Lord has given us in these two sacraments of union and communion! Our reception of our spouse enriches our life-giving love; our reception of our Lord in the Eucharist makes our love fruitful. All of this is part of God's plan to restore our communion with Him and prepare us for eternity.

Kimberly Hahn is an internationally known speaker and author. Along with her husband Scott, she is coauthor of Rome, Sweet Home *(Ignatius Press), which chronicles their celebrated conversion to the Catholic faith. She is also the author of* Life-Giving Love *(Servant) and coauthor with Mary Hasson of* Catholic Education: Homeward Bound *(Ignatius Press).*

Bibliography

Aquilina, Mike. *The Mass of the Early Christians*. Huntington, IN.: Our Sunday Visitor, 2001.

Aquilina, Mike, and Regis Flaherty. *The How-To Book of Catholic Devotions: Everything You Need to Know but No One Ever Taught You*. Huntington, IN: Our Sunday Visitor, 2000.

Barker, Margaret. "The Temple Roots of the Liturgy."As reprinted on the University of Marquette's Web site (www.marquette.edu/maqom/roots).

Catechism of the Catholic Church. Second Edition. Washington, DC: United States Catholic Conference, Inc.—Libreria Editrice Vaticana, 1997.

The Catechism of the Council of Trent. Translated by Rev. John A. McHugh, O.P., and Charles J. Callan, O.P. Rockford, IL: TAN Books, 1982.

Scripture and the Mystery of the Family of God. Edited by Scott Hahn and Leon Suprenant. Steubenville, OH: Emmaus Road, 1998.

Scripture and the Mystery of the Mother of God. Edited by Leon Suprenant. Steubenville, OH: Emmaus Road, 2000.

Cavins, Jeff. *My Life on the Rock*. E3Press, 2000. Revised edition, Encinatas, CA: Ascension Press, 2003.

Cavins, Jeff and Matt Pinto. *Amazing Grace for the Catholic Heart*. West Chester, PA: Ascension Press, 2003.

———. *Amazing Grace for Those Who Suffer*. West Chester, PA: Ascension Press, 2002.

Council of Trent. Decree Concerning the Most Holy
    Sacrament of the Eucharist. October, 1551. In *The
    Canons and Decrees of the Council of Trent*.
    Translated by Rev. H. J. Schroeder O.P. Rockford,
    IL: TAN Books, 1978.
Daniélou, Jean Cardinal, S.J. *The Bible and the
    Liturgy*. Notre Dame, IN: University of Notre
    Dame Press, 1956.
———. *From Shadows to Reality: Studies in the
    Biblical Typology of the Fathers*. London: Burns
    and Oates, 1960.
Daube, David. *The New Testament and Rabbinic
    Judaism*. Peabody, MA: Hendrickson Publishers,
    1956.
Duggan, Michael. *The Consuming Fire: A Christian
    Introduction to the Old Testament*. San Francisco:
    Ignatius Press, 1991.
Durrwell, Francois-Xavier, C.ss.R., "Eucharist and
    Parousia." *Lumen Vitae* 26 (1971): 273–315.
Gese, Hartmut. *Essays on Biblical Theology*. Translated
    by Keith Crim. Minneapolis: Augsburg, 1981.
Gihr, Rev. Dr. Nicholas. *The Holy Sacrifice of the
    Mass: Dogmatically, Liturgically, and Ascetically
    Explained*. Translated from the German. St. Louis:
    B. Herder Book Co., 1949.
Gray, Tim. *Mission of the Messiah: On the Gospel of
    Luke*. Steubenville, OH: Emmaus Road, 1998.
———. *Sacraments in Scripture: Salvation History
    Made Present*. Steubenville, OH: Emmaus Road,
    2001.
Groeschel, Rev. Benedict J. and James Monti. *In the
    Presence of Our Lord: A History, Theology, and
    Psychology of Eucharistic Devotion*. Huntington,
    IN: Our Sunday Visitor, 1997.

Hahn, Kimberly. *Life-Giving Love: Embracing God's Beautiful Design for Marriage*. Ann Arbor, MI: Servant Books, 2001.

Hahn, Scott. *A Father Who Keeps His Promises: God's Covenant Love in Scripture*. Ann Arbor, MI: Servant Books, 1998.

———. *The Lamb's Supper: The Mass as Heaven on Earth*. New York: Doubleday, 1999.

Hahn, Scott, and Curtis Mitch. *Ignatius Catholic Study Bible: The Gospel of Matthew*. San Francisco: Ignatius Press, 2000.

———. *Ignatius Catholic Study Bible: The Gospel of John*. San Francisco: Ignatius Press, 2003.

Hays, Richard B. *Echoes of Scripture in the Letters of Paul*. New Haven and London: Yale University Press, 1989.

Hayward, Robert. "The Present State of Research into the Targumic Account of the Sacrifice of Isaac." *Journal of Jewish Studies* 32 (August 1981).

Howard, Thomas. *If Your Mind Wanders at Mass*. Steubenville, OH: Franciscan University Press, 1995.

Jeremias, Rev. Joachim. *The Eucharistic Words of Jesus*. Translated by Rev. Arnold Ehrhardt, Oxford: Basil Blackwell, 1955.

Journey with the Fathers: Commentaries on the Sunday Gospels. Edited by Edith Barnecut, O.S.B. 3 vols. New Rochelle, NY: New City Press, 1992.

Jungmann, Rev. Josef A., S.J. *The Mass: An Historical, Theological, and Pastoral Survey*. Translated by Rev. Julian Fernandes, S.J. Edited by Mary Ellen Evans. Collegeville, MN: The Liturgical Press, 1976.

————. *The Mass of the Roman Rite: Its Origins and Development*. Allen, TX: Christian Classics, 1986 (replica edition).

Keating, Karl. *Catholicism and Fundamentalism*. San Francisco: Ignatius Press, 1988.

Kippley, John F. *Sex and the Marriage Covenant: A Basis for Morality*. Cincinnati, OH: Couple to Couple League, 1991.

————. *Marriage Is For Keeps: Foundations for Christian Marriage*. Cincinnati, OH: Foundation of the Family, 1994.

León-Dufour, Rev. Xavier., S.J. *Sharing the Eucharistic Bread: The Witness of the New Testament*. Translated by Matthew J. O'Connell. Mahwah, NJ: Paulist Press, 1987.

Likoudis, James, and Kenneth D. Whitehead. *The Pope, the Council, and the Mass*. West Hanover, MA.: The Christopher Publishing House, 1981.

Meagher, Rev. James. *How Christ Said the First Mass*. New York: Christian Press Association, 1906. Reprint Rockford, IL: TAN Books and Publishers, 1984.

O'Connor, Rev. James, *Hidden Manna: A Theology of the Eucharist*. San Francisco: Ignatius Press, 1988.

Pimentel, Stephen. *Witnesses of the Messiah: On the Acts of the Apostles 1–15*. Steubenville, OH: Emmaus Road, 2002.

Pope John Paul II. Encyclical on the Eucharist in Its Relationship to the Church *Ecclesia de Eucharistia*. April 17, 2003.

————. Encyclical Letter on the Value and Inviolability of Human Life *Evangelium Vitae*. March 25, 1994.

Pope Paul VI. Encyclical on the Holy Eucharist *Mysterium Fidei*. September 3, 1965.

Ratzinger, Joseph Cardinal. *God Is Near Us: The Eucharist, the Heart of Life*. San Francisco: Ignatius Press, 2003.

———. *A New Song for the Lord: Faith in Christ and Liturgy Today*. Translated by Martha M. Matesich. New York: A Crossroad Herder Book, The Crossroad, 1997.

———. *The Spirit of the Liturgy*. San Francisco: Ignatius Press, 2000.

Ray, Stephen K. *Crossing the Tiber: Evangelical Protestants Discover the Historic Church*. San Francisco: Ignatius Press, 1997.

Scheeben, Matthias Joseph. *The Mysteries of Christianity*. Translated by Cyril Vollert, S.J. St. Louis; London: B. Herder, 1946.

Second Vatican Council. Constitution on the Sacred Liturgy *Sacrosanctum Concilium*. December 4, 1963.

Shea, Mark. *This Is My Body: An Evangelical Discovers the Real Presence*. Front Royal, VA: Christendom Press, 1993.

Sheed, Frank. *Theology and Sanity*, 2nd ed. Huntington, IN.: Our Sunday Visitor, 1978.

———. *Theology for Beginners*. Ann Arbor, MI: Servant Books, 1982.

———. *What Difference Does Jesus Make?* Huntington, IN: Our Sunday Visitor, 1974.

Sheen, Archbishop Fulton J. *Calvary and the Mass*. New York: P.J. Kenedy & Sons, 1936; re-typeset and republished by Coalition in Support of Ecclesia Dei, in 1996.

Swetnam, Rev. James, S.J. "Christology and the Eucharist in the Epistle to the Hebrews." *Biblicum* 70 (1989), no. 1.

Van Hoye, Albert, S.J. *Old Testament Priests and the New Priest: According to the New Testament.* Translated by J. Bernard Orchard, O.S.B. Petersham, MA: St. Bede's Publications, 1986.

Vonier, Abbot Anscar. *A Key to the Doctrine of the Eucharist.* Reprint, Zaccheus Press, 2003.

Wright, N. T. *What Saint Paul Really Said: Was Paul of Tarsus the Real Founder of Christianity?* Grand Rapids: William B. Eerdmans Publishing Company, 1997.

Zolli, Eugenio. *The Nazarene.* Translated by Cyril Vollert. New Hope, KY: Urbi et Orbi/Remnant of Israel, 1999.